english for international banking

Published 1984 by
UNWIN HYMAN LIMITED
15-17 Broadwick Street
London W1V 1FP

First published by CEEL 1978
First published in this edition by Evans Brothers Limited 1979
Reprinted 1983, 1984, 1986, 1988

This edition is not for sale in Switzerland and Mexico

Printed and bound in Great Britain by
Biddles Ltd, Guildford and King's Lynn

ISBN 0 7135 2475 8

Contents

Introduction

This book has been written for intermediate and advanced students who need English for consultations with bank clients.

There are two books in this series:

1 *English for Bank Cashiers* deals with those situations met with every day at the counter of a bank.
2 *English for International Banking* deals with those situations met with in private consultations in the bank.

Since this book teaches consultation techniques and language, the best way to use it is with someone who needs the language for the same reason that you do. In this way, you can practise the dialogues, play roles and do the exercises together.
Several of the conversations have been set in Switzerland. This seemed reasonable, in view of the importance of Swiss banking in world business.
The book is accompanied by a cassette with recordings of the dialogues.
We should like to thank the Swiss Bank Corporation in Geneva, for all the help and professional advice which they gave while the book was being prepared, and also Ed Stephenson, who read the manuscripts and gave advice on American usage.

Nicolas Ferguson
Máire O'Reilly

Note on British and American usage and on using current information

British	*American*
cheque	check
cheque-book	checkbook
counter	window
criticise	criticize
current account	checking account
deposit account	savings account
haven't got	don't have
instalments	installments
long-term	long term
metre	meter

These words are marked with an asterisk (*) the first time they occur in the text.
Differences in phraseology are explained in footnotes in the text.
Interest rates etc. vary from time to time. Use current information when role playing.

1 Short-term investments

Objective: To enable you to give a description of different types of short-term investment and to answer questions on possibilities of investment.

Pre-test

Fill in each space with the appropriate word or words.

1 I've recently ——— a small amount of capital.

2 If you want your wife to withdraw money from your account, you can give her ———.

3 I'd like to ——— some money in my account, please.

4 With this account you can ——— up to $2,000 a month.

5 If you want a cheque-book*, you can open a ———.

6 I can block some of my capital, but I'd like the rest ——— at short notice.

7 For your investment, I'll ask our investment department to make you a ———.

8 Is there any ——— to the amount I can withdraw at any one time?

9 A power of attorney on your account is ———, even after your death.

10 Does a deposit account ——— me to a cheque-book?

When you've finished, turn over the page and check how many you got correct. Note down your mark. You'll need to refer to it later in order to compare it with the mark on your post-test.

Answers to Pre-test

1 I've recently acquired a small amount of capital.

2 If you want your wife to withdraw money from your account, you can give her power of attorney.

3 I'd like to deposit some money in my account, please.

4 With this account you can withdraw up to $2,000 a month.

5 If you want a cheque-book, you can open a current account*.

6 I can block some of my capital, but I'd like the rest available at short notice.

7 For your investment, I'll ask our investment department to make you a proposal.

8 Is there any limit to the amount I can withdraw at any one time?

9 A power of attorney on your account is valid, even after your death.

10 Does a deposit account entitle me to a cheque-book?

Case 1: Short-term investments

Peter Finbury visits the bank. He has $200,000 capital that he'd like to invest. He wants $50,000 immediately available at short notice, $80,000 at 4 to 5 years, and the rest can be invested at long term. He also wants to give his wife, Helen, power of attorney.

The manager, Walter Watson, has several possibilities to offer: a current account at $\frac{1}{2}$% with the possibility of immediate withdrawal; a deposit account* at $3\frac{1}{2}$% offering the possibility of withdrawing $10,000 immediately, and larger amounts with 3 months' notice; certificates of deposit at $6\frac{1}{4}$% for fixed periods of 3, 4 or 5 years; and finally, long-term investments with terms depending on a proposal from the investment department.

Role-playing Exercise

Two people take the roles of Finbury and Watson, and act out the case.

Dialogue

Listen to the recording until you understand it, without looking at the text. The terminology on pages 6 and 7 will help you.

Second Role-playing Exercise

Two people take the roles of Finbury and Watson, and act out the dialogue without the help of the tape-recording.

Text and Programmed Exercise

Look at the text. When you're sure you have no problem understanding it, turn to page 8.

Watson Good morning, sir.

Finbury Good morning.

Watson What can I do for you?

Finbury I've recently acquired a small amount of capital and I'd like to find out about investing it.

Watson In order to advise you, may I ask what your profession is, what your plans are, the term of your investment, and above all, the sum you have at your disposal.

Finbury Yes, but I'd just like some general information on investments first. My capital . . . um . . . I don't want to block all my capital. I may need some of it one of these days . . . I'd like to invest . . . half the capital, say, and have the rest at my immediate disposal. Let's say, I'd invest in the order of 200,000.

Watson Good. How soon would you like to have access to your capital once it's been invested?

Finbury Well, er . . . that depends a little on my car. I'd like to get a new one in a couple of years. I also plan to take a holiday abroad in a year's time. The rest can remain blocked.

Watson You've got several possibilities, then. First, a current account, which you know about, which pays a very small interest of ½%.

Finbury That's very little.

Watson Yes, of course. You have a second possibility, which is a deposit account. This pays 3½% . . . less tax. It also entitles you to a cheque-book. You can withdraw up to 10,000 a month. Larger sums need 3 months' notice.

Finbury And . . . er . . . can I deposit any sum?

Watson Yes, there's no limit. What I suggest, in fact, is that you open a deposit account with enough in it to cover your immediate needs. As for the rest, we can ask our investment department to make you a proposal.

Finbury That's interesting. But I'm not sure. I'll need 40,000 to 50,000 at short notice. I'd like to invest in the order of . . . er . . . 80,000 in a long-term investment and I'd like to have the remaining 80,000 available at, say, 4 to 5 years' notice.

Watson	In that case, we can offer you our certificates of deposit at 3, 4 or 5 years.
Finbury	Mmm.
Watson	And the interest is higher than on a deposit account. They pay $6\frac{1}{4}$%.
Finbury	That's interesting. If I give my wife power of attorney, would that be valid on all my accounts?
Watson	Certainly. And it remains valid even after your death.
Finbury	Mmm. Then, I'd like you to send me a proposal for investment. Meanwhile, I'd like to open a deposit account as you suggest, and I'd like to put in 50,000. We'll see about the rest later.
Watson	How much would you like in certificates of deposit?
Finbury	Oh, say, 80,000.
Watson	So, 50,000 in a deposit account, 80,000 in certificates of deposit, and we can send you a proposal for the remainder.
Finbury	That's right.
Watson	Can I ask you for some details so that I can fill in these forms. First of all, your name's Finbury. (writes) And your first name . . .?
Finbury	Peter.
Watson	Your profession?
Finbury	Um . . . author.
Watson	Your address?
Finbury	15 Church Street.
Watson	Your wife's name is . . .?
Finbury	Helen.
Watson	. . . and her maiden name?
Finbury	Setton.

Watson	Here's the form for the opening of an account. If you could sign it here . . . and here. . . . Thank you. And could I have a specimen of your signature here, please. . . . Thank you.
Finbury	Do you need my wife's signature?
Watson	Yes. Possibly you could ask her to come with you the next time you come to the bank.
Finbury	Fine.
Watson	Could I have your passport, please? . . . Thank you. All right. Let's go over to the counter* and you can deposit the 50,000.
Finbury	Certainly.

Terminology

account	What kind of *account* have you got?
acquired	I've recently *acquired* a small amount of capital.
amount	I can only invest a small *amount* at long-term.
at your disposal	I'd like to invest part of my capital, and have the rest *at my immediate disposal*.
available	With a current account, your money is immediately *available*.
block	I'll need $5,000 available at short notice, and I can *block* the rest.
capital	I'd like to invest my *capital* in bonds.
certificate of deposit	We can give you *certificates of deposit* for $10,000.
cheque-book (UK)	I use my *cheque-book* regularly to pay bills.
counter (UK)	I work at *counter* number six at the head office.
deposit	I'd like to *deposit* some money in my account, please.
deposit account	Our *deposit accounts* give 3½% interest.
entitle	A current account *entitles* you to a cheque-book.
have access to	I'd like to *have access to* $50,000 in about 3 years.
interest	The *interest* on a current account is only ½%.
invest	I'd like to *invest* part of my capital in shares.
investment	I'd like an *investment* which pays a good interest.
investment department	Can your *investment department* send me a proposal?

limit	A deposit account *limits* the amount you can withdraw at any one time.
long-term	Bonds are a *long-term* investment.
power of attorney	If you give your wife *power of attorney,* she can withdraw money from your account.
proposal	The terms of a long-term investment depend on a *proposal* from the investment department.
short notice	I'd like $10,000 available at *short notice*; for example, within about two weeks
sign	Could you *sign* the back of this cheque*, please?
signature	If you want to give your wife power of attorney, we'll need a copy of her *signature*.
sum	What *sum* have you got to invest?
tax	Our deposit accounts pay 3½% interest, less *tax*.
term	The *terms* depend on the investment department's proposal.
valid	A power of attorney is *valid* even after your death.

Programmed Exercise

The following exercise has been programmed. There are a number of questions presented in the following manner.

Question

. . .

Answer

Using a piece of cardboard as a mask, slip the cardboard down the page to the first dotted line. Then, on another piece of paper, write down the answer to the first question. Very often the answer to the question you are doing is higher up on the page. Don't look back. When you've answered the first question, slip the cardboard down to uncover the answer; then check what you've written. If you find that your answer isn't correct, look back and see if you can find where you went wrong before going on to the next question.

Work progressively through the programme. The questions have been planned in such a way that each one will help the next.

Don't write on the programme itself, as you may want to do it again at a later stage.

If you're working with another student, when you've finished writing the programme, one of you can take the book and ask the other the questions. It's very important not to read directly from the book, as this tends to destroy your rhythm. First look at the question in the book; then look at your partner and, without looking back at the book, ask the question. When one student has finished, you can swop roles.

Finally, you can close your book and continue asking and answering the questions without help.

Finbury If I give my wife power of attorney, would that be valid on all my accounts?
Watson Certainly. And it remains valid even after your death.

1 If Mr Finbury gives his wife power of attorney, what accounts would it be valid on?

. . .

On all of them.

2 Ask Watson what accounts Mrs Finbury's power of attorney would be valid on.

. . .

What accounts would Mrs Finbury's power of attorney be valid on?

3 Ask Watson what would happen after Finbury's death if he gave his wife power of attorney.

. . .

What would happen after Finbury's death if he gave his wife power of attorney?

4 What happens after his death?

. . .

The power of attorney remains valid.

5 Ask Watson how long a power of attorney remains valid for.

. . .

How long does a power of attorney remain valid for?

Finbury Then I'd like you to send me a proposal for investment.

6 What would Finbury like the bank to send him?

. . .

A proposal for investment.

7 Ask Finbury what kind of proposal he'd like the bank to send him.

. . .

What kind of proposal would you like the bank to send you?

8 What kind of proposal would he like the bank to send him?

. . .

A proposal for investment.

9 Does Finbury plan to come to the bank to collect the proposal?

. . .

No, he'd like the bank to send it to him.

Finbury Meanwhile, I'd like to open a deposit account as you suggest, and I'd like to put in 50,000. We'll see about the rest later.

10 Ask Finbury what kind of account he'd like to open

. . .

What kind of account would you like to open?

11 Did Finbury plan to open a deposit account before he visited Watson?

. . .

No. (Watson suggested it.)

12 Ask Finbury how much he'd like to put into the account.

. . .

How much would like to put into the account?

13 How much would he like to put in?

. . .

50,000.

14 What about the rest of his capital?

. . .

He'll see about it later.

Watson How much would you like in certificates of deposit?
Finbury Oh, say, 80,000.
Watson So, 50,000 in a deposit account, and 80,000 in certificates of deposit, and we can send you a proposal for the remainder.
Finbury That's right.

15 Ask Watson how much Finbury wants in certificates of deposit.

. . .

How much does Finbury want in certificates of deposit?

16 Finbury wants 80,000 in certificates of deposit, and 50,000 in a deposit account. Is that all?

. . .

No. The bank can send him a proposal for the remainder.

You've just done 16 questions. If you got 3 or more wrong, do them again. If you got 2 or less wrong, you can continue with the exercise on the next page.

Vocabulary Exercise 1

Complete each space in the following text with the word or words you consider most appropriate.

Watson	You've got several ———, then. First, a current account, which you know about, which ——— a very small ——— of ½%.
Finbury	That's very little.
Watson	Yes, of course. You have a second ———, which is a ———. This ——— 3½% . . . less ———. It also ——— you to a ———. You can ——— up to 10,000 a month. Larger ——— need 3 months' ———.
Finbury	And . . . er . . . can I ——— any sum?
Watson	Yes, there's no ———. What I suggest, in fact, is that you open a ——— with enough in it to ——— your immediate needs. As for the rest, we can ask our ——— to make you a ———.
Finbury	That's interesting. But I'm not sure. I'll need 40,000 to 50,000 at ———. I'd like to ——— in the order of . . . er . . . 80,000 in a ——— investment and I'd like to have the remaining 80,000 ——— at, say, 4 to 5 years' ———.
Watson	In that case, we can offer you our ——— at 3, 4 or 5 years.
Finbury	Mmm.
Watson	And the ——— is higher than on a ———. They ——— 6¼%.
Finbury	That's interesting.

When you've finished, turn back to pages 4 and 5 and correct what you've done. Calculate the number you had correct, and then use the following table to interpret your result.

28 or more correct	Excellent
Between 25 and 27 correct	Good
Between 22 and 24 correct	Fair. Study the original dialogue again before going on.

Vocabulary Exercise 2

Complete each blank space with the appropriate word or words.

If you want to ——— money at ———, you've got several ———: first, a ———. This gives you the possibility of having all your money ——— immediate ———. It also ——— you to a cheque-book. However, it only gives ½% ———.

Second, you've got a ———, which usually pays about 3½% ———, less ———. In that respect, a ———'s a better ——— than a ———. However, though you are ——— to a ———, you can only ——— up to a certain ——— each month. For larger ———, you must give the ——— a few months' ———.

Finally, you have ———. These pay in the order of 6½% ———. However, they ——— your ——— for a ——— of 3, 4 or 5 years.

Your choice of ——— investment, therefore, will depend largely on how quickly you'd like to ——— your money.

When you've finished, turn over the page and check what you've done. Calculate the number you had correct, then use the following table to interpret your result.

25 or more correct	Excellent
Between 21 and 23 correct	Good
Between 17 and 20 correct	Fair. Study the original dialogue before going on.

If you want to invest money at short term, you've got several possibilities: first, a current account. This gives you the possibility of having all your money at your immediate disposal. It also entitles you to a cheque-book. However, it only gives ½% interest.

Second, you've got a deposit account, which usually pays about 3½% interest, less tax. In that respect, a deposit account's a better investment than a current account. However, though you are entitled to a cheque-book, you can only withdraw up to a certain sum each month. For larger amounts, you must give the bank a few months' notice.

Finally, you have certificates of deposit. These pay in the order of 6½% interest. However, they block your capital for a fixed period of 3, 4 or 5 years.

Your choice of short-term investment, therefore, will depend largely on how quickly you'd like to have access to your money.

Post-test

Fill in each blank space with the appropriate word or words.

1 I'll need forty to fifty thousand at ———.

2 I'd like to find out about investing a small ——— of capital.

3 How soon would you like to ——— to your capital once it's been invested?

4 If you tell me what sum you have at ———, I can advise you how to invest it.

5 With a deposit account, you can ——— up to 10,000 a month.

6 Both deposit and current accounts ——— you to a cheque-book.

7 There's no ——— to the amount you can put into your account.

8 Can your investment department send me a ——— for investing my money?

9 Would my wife's power of attorney be ——— on all my accounts?

10 With a current account, you can ——— your money without notice.

If you're not sure of any of the answers, look back and check. The fact that you're not sure is as serious as if you were wrong. The answers to this post-test are not given in this book. It's up to you.

2 The form of a consultation

Objective: To examine the sequence of a consultation.

The form of a consultation

The conversation between Mr Watson and Mr Finbury, like most consultations in a bank, was of the following form.

1 *Establishing contact.* The manager or assistant manager first establishes contact with his customer, greeting him and putting him at his ease. This is done politely, but with neither effusiveness or familiarity.

2 *Finding out what the person wants.* It's necessary to find out what the client wants.

3 *Giving information.* Information is given concisely, vividly and clearly. Moreover, it is adapted to the listener's viewpoint.

4 *Arguing the point.* The client is persuaded to do something.

5 *Taking down details in writing.* Very often it will be necessary to fill in a form or take notes.

6 *Conclusion and thanks.* The manager reaffirms his readiness to help.

Look at the text of the dialogue on pp. 4-6, and mark where each section begins and ends.

Case 2: A short consultation

The following dialogue recently took place in a small private consulting room in a provincial bank. It is an example of what should *not* happen during a bank consultation.

Martin Hatfield has recently acquired $10,000 and he'd like to find out about short-term investments. Peter Wills gives some information.

Evaluate the six parts of the consultation, and give your reasons why the conversation was positive or not.

Wills	Good morning. Have a seat, please.
Hatfield	My name's Martin Hatfield. I've recently acquired a small amount of capital and I'd like to find out about investing it.
Wills	How much?
Hatfield	In the order of $10,000.
Wills	Hmm. That's not too much. They could have told you downstairs. Anyway, here's the list of accounts and their interest rates. There's a wide range, as you can see. We have current accounts at $\frac{1}{2}$%, deposit accounts at $3\frac{1}{2}$%, certificates of deposit at 6 to $6\frac{1}{4}$%, and you could also consult our Investment Department for a long-term investment.
Hatfield	That's very good. You seem to have more possibilities than most banks.
Wills	Mmm. That's possible.
Hatfield	The certificates of deposit seem interesting.
Wills	Oh, yes. They're a possibility. They pay 6% for 3 to 4 years, and $6\frac{1}{4}$% for 5 years or more.
Hatfield	It's difficult to decide. I don't want to block my money for too long, so you see 5 years seems to present a difficulty.

Wills Well, it's up to you, really.

Hatfield Well, I'll think about it. Thank you.

Wills That's all right.

Role-playing Exercise

Two people take the roles of Martin Hatfield and Peter Wills, and act out a better consultation than the one given.

3 Investment: bonds and shares

Objective: To enable you to explain what bonds, shares and investment funds are.

Pre-test

Fill in the spaces with the appropriate word or words.

1 The bank can give you a loan with your life insurance policy as ———.

2 If you buy ——— in a company, you become, in a manner of speaking, an owner of the company.

3 I think you could invest 40% of your ——— in a fund.

4 Can you give me a ——— against bonds?

5 You certainly run a greater ——— with shares than with bonds.

6 We can make you up a portfolio in shares and bonds in carefully calculated ———.

7 Becoming the owner of a ——— in an investment fund, you limit your risks.

8 Have I got the same ——— of movement with bonds as with shares?

9 There's ½% difference in the interest ———.

10 I run a risk if I sell my bonds before they come to ———.

When you've finished, turn over the page and check how many you got correct. Note down your mark. You'll need to refer to it later.

Answers to Pre-test

1 The bank can give you a loan with your life insurance policy as collateral.

2 If you buy shares[1] in a company, you become, in a manner of speaking, an owner of the company.

3 I think you could invest 40% of your assets in a fund.

4 Can you give me a loan against bonds?

5 You certainly run a greater risk with shares than with bonds.

6 We can make you up a portfolio in shares and bonds in carefully calculated proportions.

7 Becoming the owner of a unit in an investment fund, you limit your risks.

8 Have I got the same freedom of movement with bonds as with shares?

9 There's ½% difference in the interest rates.

10 I run a risk if I sell my bonds before they come to maturity.

[1]US: *stock*

Case 3: Investment: bonds and shares

Peter Finch, a bank consultant, speaks to Bob Parkins. Mr Parkins has £40,000 that he's been advised to invest, and he'd like some information.

Mr Finch explains what bonds and shares are, and what security and profit they give. He also mentions investment funds.

Mr Parkins says he will think things over.

Role-playing Exercise

Two people take the roles of Peter Finch and Bob Parkins and act out the case.

Dialogue

Now listen to the tape-recording until you understand it without looking at the text. The terminology on page 25 will help you.

The Form of the Interview

Using the text, divide the interview up into sections as was shown on page 16. Then evaluate each part.

Second Role-playing Exercise

Two people take the roles of Peter Finch and Bob Parkins again, and act out the dialogue without the help of the tape-recording.

Text and Programmed Exercise

When you've finished, turn to the page after the terminology and do the programmed exercise.

Finch	Good morning.
Parkins	I'd like some advice, please. I've got a certain amount of money that I've been advised to invest. I've been told about bonds and shares . . . um . . . but I really don't know anything about banking and I'd like to ask . . . um . . . to ask you all about it.
Finch	First, I'd like to ask you how much capital you have at your disposal and what your plans are. Do you want to put something aside for your retirement, or do you think you'll need funds at short notice. . .?
Parkins	Well, part is savings and part is an inheritance that I've just received. In all, about £40,000. At the moment, most is in deposit accounts spread around various banks.
Finch	Well, I think it's certainly in your interest to consolidate your capital in one bank. We can, if you wish, replace part of it by bonds. In other words, you lend your money to an organization for a fixed period at a fixed interest rate. The organization promises to repay you in the agreed term, and meanwhile pays you a yearly interest.
Parkins	Is the interest higher than on a deposit account?
Finch	Yes, certainly. Bonds are issued for periods from 15 years upwards, and a long-term investment generally pays more.
Parkins	Can I withdraw my money whenever I want?
Finch	You can ask us to sell your bonds for you. Their value will depend on the market at the time. It might be higher than you bought at, or it might be lower. That depends on the market – if it's on the rise or not. In fact, fluctuation of the value of bonds is never very great – not as great as in the case of shares, for example.
Parkins	Yes .. . um, there's something I don't quite understand. You say the interest rate is higher than on my savings accounts, but if I want to use my money, I must sell my bonds.
Finch	Yes, if you want to use your money before the bonds come to maturity. Alternatively, the bank can give you a loan with the bonds as collateral. For example, the bank might lend you 80% of the value of the bonds on the stock exchange at the moment you ask for the loan.

Parkins — If I've understood correctly, I can't use my money – your loan is limited – and I run a risk of loss if I want to sell before maturity.

Finch — Certainly, you run a certain risk.

Parkins — In other words, if I want to be sure of seeing my capital again, I must wait for maturity.

Finch — Exactly.

Parkins — And what about shares . . . are the risks the same?

Finch — If you buy shares[1] in a company, you become, in a manner of speaking, the owner of the company, together with a lot of other people. Bonds give you a fixed interest, while a share gives you an interest[2] depending on the success of the company. Shares, however, ensure you against devaluation.

Parkins — That's a bit complicated. Can you advise me regularly . . . tell me when I should buy and sell?

Finch — We've got specialists who deal with all that. However, you certainly run a greater risk with shares than with bonds. If you have 40,000 to invest, we'd probably advise you to invest a maximum of a third of that in shares. The rest should be invested in bonds or in certificates of deposit, for example. In this way, you can limit your risks.

Parkins — Yes. Of course, you understand, when you've worked hard all your life to save a small sum, you don't want to invest it in just anything.

Finch — I presume, then, you would like to have security more than a profit.

Parkins — Well, one needn't necessarily rule out the other (laugh). It's up to you to advise me.

Finch — We also have investment funds, which banks administer. We administer several, and we can make you up a portfolio in shares and bonds in carefully calculated proportions. Becoming the

[1] Strictly speaking, one buys stock in a company, or one buys a certain number of units of the company's stock (10, 20, 40). (Shares are thus a measure of stock.)
[2] Strictly speaking, a share does not give interest, but pays a dividend.

owner of a unit, you limit your risk. You have a share in the repayment of the bonds in the fund that also holds shares, so that, in addition, you benefit from the profit that the shares produce. I think you could invest 40% of your assets in a fund.

Parkins How can I control my investment in such a case? Have I got the same freedom of movement as with shares?

Finch Certainly. They are negotiable whenever you like. The rates are fixed daily, so that you can sell whenever you wish. Of course, you won't be able to avoid the ups and downs of the market.

Parkins Yes. I see.

Finch In this way, you can benefit from a larger range of both bonds and shares.

Parkins In other words, I diversify my risk.

Finch Exactly.

Parkins One thing interests me. In speaking of bonds just now, you said that your bank could give me a loan against bonds. In such a case, what are the conditions? Is the interest rate on a loan higher than on the bonds?

Finch Yes. There's between $\frac{1}{2}$ and 1% difference in the rates. After all, the bank has to live.

Parkins Of course. Well, thank you. I wanted above all to know about the difference between bonds and shares. I think I've understood now. I'd like to talk everything over with my wife, and I'll come back to see you again.

Finch Why not come with your wife? I'd be happy to meet her and to explain everything as I have just done with you.

Parkins That's very kind. Could I have your name and telephone number, then?

Finch My name is Peter Finch, and my number is 224.644.

Parkins Goodbye, then.

Finch I'll just show you the way.

Terminology

assets	You could invest 40%of your *assets* in a fund.
bond	What's the present value of my *bonds*?
collateral	We can give you a loan with your bonds as *collateral*.
consolidate	I'd like to *consolidate* my capital in one bank.
diversify	I'd like both bonds and shares, to *diversify* my risk.
dividend	Bonds pay interest; shares pay *dividends*.
fixed period	Bonds are issued for a *fixed period*, usually from 15 years up.
fixed rate	With bonds, you lend your money at a *fixed rate*.
fluctuation	The *fluctuation* of the value of bonds is never very great.
funds	I'll certainly need some *funds* at short notice.
inheritance	This money is part of my *inheritance*.
investment fund	The bank administers an *investment fund*.
issue	Bonds are *issued* for periods of 15 years or more.
loan	The bank can give you a *loan* with your bonds as collateral.
loss	You risk a *loss* if you sell your bonds now.
market	Sell your bonds now; the *market* is very good.
maturity	My bonds won't reach *maturity* for another six years.
negotiable	Bonds are *negotiable* whenever you like.
portfolio	We can prepare you a *portfolio* in bonds and shares.
rate	What would the *rate* of interest be in this investment?
risk (n)	There's a bigger *risk* with shares than with bonds.
risk (v)	You *risk* a loss if you sell your bonds now.
savings	This money is all our *savings*, so I'd like security first.
share	If you have *shares* in a company, you are a part owner of that company.
stock exchange	We can lend you 80% of the value of your bonds on the *stock exchange*.
value (n)	What's the present *value* of my bonds?

Programmed Exercise

Finch I think it's certainly in your interest to consolidate your capital in one bank. We can, if you wish, replace part of it by bonds.

1 What does Finch think it's in Parkins' interest to do?

. . .

To centralize his capital in one bank.

2 What can the bank do with Parkins' capital?

. . .

Replace part of it by bonds.

3 Ask Finch what they can replace part of the capital by.

. . .

What can you replace part of the capital by?

4 What can the bank do with part of the capital?

. . .

They can replace it by bonds.

Finch In other words, you lend your money to an organization for a fixed period at a fixed interest rate. The organization promises to repay you in the agreed term, and meanwhile pays you a yearly interest.

5 When you buy bonds, what do you do for a fixed period at a fixed interest rate?

. . .

You lend your money to an organization.

6 When you lend your money to an organization, what is fixed?

. . .

The period and the interest rate.

7 Ask Finch what happens when a person buys bonds?

. . .

What happens when a person buys bonds?

8 What happens when a person buys bonds?

. . .

He lends his money to an organization for a fixed period at a fixed interest rate.

Parkins Is the interest higher than on a deposit account?
Finch Yes, certainly. Bonds are issued for periods from 15 years upwards . . . and a long-term investment generally pays more.

9 What can you say about the interest on bonds?

. . .

It's higher than on a deposit account.

10 How long are bonds issued for?

. . .

For periods from 15 years upwards.

11 What can you say about bonds?

. . .

They're issued for periods from 15 years upwards, and the interest is higher than on a deposit account.

12 Why is the interest on bonds higher than on a deposit account?

. . .

Because a long-term investment generally pays more.

13 Ask Finch how long bonds are normally issued for.

. . .

How long are bonds normally issued for?

14 Ask him why the interest on bonds is higher than on a deposit account.

. . .

Why is the interest on bonds higher than on a deposit account?

You've just answered 14 questions. If you got 2 or more wrong, do them again. If you got 1 or less wrong, go on to the next page.

Vocabulary Exercise 1

Complete each space with the appropriate word or words.

Finch — If you buy ——— in a company, you become, in a manner of speaking, the ——— of the company, together with a lot of other people. ——— give you a ———, while a ——— gives you an ——— depending on the ——— of the company. ———, however, ——— you against ———.

Parkins — That's a bit complicated. Can you ——— me regularly . . . tell me what I should ——— and sell?

Finch — We've got ——— who deal with all that. However, you certainly run a greater ——— with ——— than with ———. If you have 40,000 to ———, we'd probably ——— you to ——— a maximum of a third of that in ———. The rest should be ——— in ——— or in ———, for example. In this way. you can ——— your ———.

Parkins — Yes. Of course, you understand when you've worked hard all your life to save a small ———, you don't want to ——— it in just anything.

Finch — I presume, then, you would like to have ——— more than a profit.

Parkins — Well, one needn't necessarily rule out the other. It's up to you to advise me.

Finch — We also have ———, which banks ———. We ——— several, and we can make you up a ——— in ——— and ——— in carefully ——— proportions. Becoming the owner of a ———, you ——— your ———. You have a ——— in the ——— of the ——— in the ——— that also holds ———, so that, in addition, you benefit from the ——— that the ——— produce. I think you could ——— 40% of your ——— in a ———.

When you've finished, turn back to pages 23 and 24 and check your answers. Then use the following table to interpret your result.

44 or more correct	Excellent
Between 40 and 43 correct	Good
Between 36 and 39 correct	Fair. Study the original dialogue again before going on.

Vocabulary Exercise 2

Complete each space with the appropriate word or words.

One way of——— your money is to buy———. This means that you lend your——— to an——— for a——— at a———. The——— promises to ——— you in the agreed———, and meanwhile, you get a yearly———.

——— are normally ——— for periods of 15 years or more, so they're ——— investments and ——— investments generally pay more than short-term.

If you need your ——— before your ——— come to ———, you can ask your ——— to sell them for you. Their ——— will then depend on the ——— at the time you decide to sell. It might be a bit higher or lower than you bought at, but the——— in the——— of——— is never very great.

You can also use your——— as——— against a——— corresponding to slightly less than their ——— on the ——— at the time you ask for the ———. Of course, the ——— rate on ——— is a little higher than that on ———.

When you've finished, turn over the page and check what you've done. Then use the following table to interpret your result.

27 or more correct	Excellent
Between 24 and 26 correct	Good
Between 21 and 23 correct	Fair. Study the original dialogue again before going on.

One way of investing your money is to buy bonds. This means that you lend your money to an organization for a fixed period at a fixed interest rate. The organization promises to repay you in the agreed term, and meanwhile, you get a yearly interest.

Bonds are normally issued for periods of 15 years or more, so they're long-term investments, and long-term investments generally pay more than short-term.

If you need your money before your bonds come to maturity, you can ask your bank to sell them for you. Their value will then depend on the market at the time you decide to sell. It might be a bit higher or lower than you bought at, but the fluctuation in the value of bonds is never very great.

You can also use your bonds as collateral against a loan corresponding to slightly less than their value on the stock exchange at the time you ask for the loan. Of course, the interest rate on loans is a little higher than that on bonds.

Post-test

1 Shares insure you against ———.

2 The bank can lend you 80% of the value of your bonds on the ———.

3 The dividend paid on ——— depends on the success of the company.

4 The ——— of the value of bonds is never very great.

5 I'd like to sell my bonds. What's the ——— like at the moment?

6 Bonds can be sold any time, and the ——— are fixed daily.

7 At the moment, my capital is spread round various banks, but I'd like to ——— it.

8 Bonds are ——— for periods from 15 years upwards.

9 Do you think you'll need ——— at short notice?

10 I think I'll take your advice. That way, I can benefit from a larger range of both bonds and shares, and ——— my risk.

If you're not sure of any of the answers, look back and check. The fact that you're not sure is as serious as if you were wrong. The answers to this post-test are not given in this book. It's up to you.

4 Small loans

Objective: To enable you to discuss a small loan with a client.

Pre-test

Fill in each blank space with the appropriate word or words.

1 We could organize a ——— against a monthly deduction from your salary.

2 I pay for my car in monthly ——— of SFr. 250.

3 Do you want to ——— the loan directly, or would you like us to arrange a deduction from your salary?

4 Could the bank give me a ——— to cover the down payment?

5 I can pay you back SFr. 3,000 in 30 days, and the ——— at the end of April.

6 I'm afraid there isn't enough in your account ——— the cheque you wrote for your car.

7 Our affiliated firm can also take out an all-risk ——— for you.

8 We could lend you up to SFr. 2,000 as your ——— is paid regularly into your account.

9 I can give you the name of a firm which ——— with matters like this.

10 We wouldn't be able to give you a personal ——— of this type.

When you've finished, turn over the page and check your answers. Keep a note of your mark, as you'll need to refer to it later in order to compare it with your mark on the post-test.

Answers to Pre-test

1 We could organize a loan against a monthly deduction from your salary.

2 I pay for my car in monthly instalments of SFr. 250.

3 Do you want to pay back (or: repay) the loan directly, or would you like us to arrange a deduction from your salary?

4 Could the bank give me a loan to cover the down payment?

5 I can pay you back SFr. 3,000 in 30 days, and the balance (or: the rest) at the end of April.

6 I'm afraid there isn't enough in your account to cover the cheque you wrote for your car.

7 Our affiliated firm can also take out an all-risk insurance (or: policy) for you.

8 We could lend you up to SFr. 2,000, as your salary is paid regularly into your account.

9 I can give you the name of a firm which deals with matters like this.

10 We wouldn't be able to give you a personal loan of this type.

Case 4: Small loans

Arthur Milton visits Mr Creed at the bank. Mr Milton wants a loan of SFr. 3,500 to cover the down payment for a new car. He's a salesman in a firm of electric home appliances, and his old car has been written off in an accident.

He has a deposit account in the bank, but with only SFr. 750 in it. He could pay back the loan at a rate of SFr. 150 a month. Creed has to refuse the loan, but suggests that Mr Milton visit Mr Wilkinson of FINLOAN, a finance firm, who could possibly lend him the necessary money against a monthly deduction from Mr Milton's salary.

Role-playing Exercise

Two people take the roles of Creed and Milton, and act out the case.

Dialogue

Now listen to the tape-recording until you understand it without looking at the text. The terminology on page 36 will help you.

The Form of an Interview

Using the text, divide the interview up into sections as shown on page 16. Then evaluate each part.

Second Role-playing Exercise

Two people take the roles of Creed and Milton, and act out the case without the help of the tape-recording.

Text and Programmed Exercise

Look at the text, and when you're sure you have no problem understanding it, turn to page 37.

Creed Good morning. What can I do for you?

Milton Good morning. My name's Milton. I've got a small account in your bank, but I need some money and what I have in my deposit account is not enough. I've had a car accident – not through my fault – but my car's been completely written off. I need a car for my job, as I have to travel a lot. I can buy one in instalments* but I have to give a down payment of SFr. 3,500 and I can't at the moment. My question is this. Can the bank give me a loan to cover the down payment?*

Creed What's the balance of your deposit account at the moment?

Milton About SFr. 750.

Creed And what's your profession?

Milton I'm a salesman in a firm of electric home appliances. I have to travel around my sales area, and I have to visit local salesmen.

Creed And you have your own car?

Milton Yes. My last one was my own, and I'd just finished paying for it.

Creed And isn't your employer prepared to help you in this particular case?

Milton Maybe he would be . . . but I'd prefer to avoid asking him.

Creed How much is the car you plan to buy?

Milton SFr. 11,200.

Creed So you have to give a down payment of SFr. 3,500.

Milton Yes.

Creed And at the moment, you only have SFr. 750.

Milton That's right.

Creed How must you pay the balance?

Milton In monthly instalments* of SFr. 215.

Creed How would you pay back the SFr. 3,500 to the bank?

Milton Monthly . . . at the rate of, say, SFr. 150 a month. I could probably manage larger payments in a few months. At the moment, however, things are a bit tight.

Creed I see. Well, I'm afraid we wouldn't be able to give you a personal loan of this type. Nevertheless, we have an affiliated firm called Finloan who deal with matters like this. They can organize a loan against a monthly deduction from your salary. They also take out an all-risk insurance for you.

Milton That's fine. I had hoped to do it directly with you, but I'll go to Finloan. (getting up).

Creed We could probably have given you an overdraft of up to, say SFr. 2,000 since your salary is paid regularly into your account, I see. Alternatively, we might have given you a short-term loan for 2–3 months – which is why I asked you all the questions. However, I'm sure Mr Wilkinson, the director of Finloan, can help you.

Milton Well, thank you. . . . Good morning.

Creed Good morning, sir.

Terminology

affiliated	Our *affiliated* firm deals with matters like this.
all-risk	Have you got an *all-risk* insurance, sir?
balance	What's the *balance* of your account at the moment?
cover	The bank can let you have a loan to *cover* the down payment.
deal with	Are you the person who *deals with* short-term loans?
deduction	I want to organize a *deduction* from my salary every month.
down payment	The *down payment* on this house is a lot, but the monthly instalments aren't very high.
finance firm	Do you know of a good *finance firm* who might be able to help?
instalments	I plan to buy a car in *instalments*.
insurance	The finance firm can take out an all-risk *insurance* for you.
overdraft	We can let you have an *overdraft* to the value of your salary.
paid	I've finally *paid* the last instalment, and the car's mine.
pay back	How do you plan to *pay back* the loan?
payment	I can probably manage larger *payments* in a few months, but at the moment I can only pay back £20 a month.
salary	My present *salary* isn't very high, though my job's very difficult.

Programmed Exercise

Creed Isn't your employer prepared to help you in this particular case?
Milton Maybe he would be . . . but I'd prefer to avoid asking him.

1 Ask Milton if he's asked his employer to help him.

. . .

Have you asked your employer to help you?

2 Is Milton's employer prepared to help him in this particular case?

. . .

Maybe he would be . . . but Milton would prefer to avoid asking him.

Creed How much is the car you plan to buy?
Milton SFr. 11,200.
Creed So, you have to give a down payment of SFr. 3,500.
Milton Yes.

3 What does Milton plan to do?

. . .

(To) buy a car.

4 Ask Milton how much the car he wants to buy is.

. . .

How much is the car you want to buy?

5 Ask Milton if he'll have to give a down payment on the new car.

. . .

Will you have to give a down payment on the new car?

6 Ask him how much the down payment on the car he plans to buy is.

. . .

How much is the down payment on the car you plan to buy?

7 How much is the down payment on the car Milton wants to buy?

. . .

SFr. 3,500.

Creed And at the moment, you only have SFr. 750.
Milton That's right.

8 Ask Milton how much he's got at the moment.

. . .

How much have you got at the moment?

9 Has Milton got a lot of money at the moment?

. . .

No. He's only got SFr. 750.

Creed How must you pay the balance?
Milton In monthly instalments of SFr. 215.

10 How much is the down payment on the car Milton wants?

. . .

SFr. 3,500.

11 And how must he pay the balance?

. . .

In monthly instalments of SFr. 215.

12 Ask Milton how much the monthly instalments on his new car will be.

. . .

How much will the monthly instalments on your new car be?

Creed How would you pay back the SFr. 3,500 to the bank?
Milton Monthly . . . at the rate of, say, SFr. 150 a month. I could probably manage larger payments in a few months. At the moment, however, things are a bit tight.

13 Ask Milton how he'd pay back the loan of SFr. 3,500.

. . .

How would you pay back the loan of SFr. 3,500?

14 How would he pay back the loan?

. . .

Monthly, at the rate of, say, SFr. 150.

15 SFr. 150 is very little. What does Milton think about that?

. . .

He'd probably be able to manage larger payments in a few months.

16 Ask Milton why he can't pay back at a higher rate just now.

. . .

Why can't you pay back at a higher rate just now?

17 Why can't he pay back at a higher rate just now?

. . .

Because things are a bit tight.

You've just answered 17 questions. If you got 3 or more wrong, do them again. If you got 2 or less wrong, go on to the next page.

Vocabulary Exercise 1

Fill in each blank space with the appropriate word or words.

Creed	How would you ——— the SFr. 3,500 to the ———?
Milton	Monthly . . . at the ——— of, say, SFr. 150 a month. I could possibly manage larger ——— in a few months. At the moment, however, things are a bit tight.
Creed	I see. Well, I'm afraid we wouldn't be able to give you a personal ——— of this type. Nevertheless, we have an ——— firm, called Finloan, who ——— with matters like this. They can ——— a ——— a monthly ——— from your ———. They can also take out an ——— for you.
Milton	That's fine. I had hoped to do it directly with you, but I'll go to Finloan.
Creed	We could probably have given you an ——— of up to, say, SFr. 2,000 since your ——— is ——— regularly into your ———, I see. Alternatively, we might have given you a ——— for 2 to 3 months. However, I'm sure Mr Wilkinson, the director of Finloan, can help you.
Milton	Well, thank you. . . . Good morning
Creed	Good morning, sir.

When you've finished, turn back to the original on page 35 and check what you've done. Then use the following table to interpret your result.

19 or more correct	Excellent
17 or 18 correct	Good
15 or 16 correct	Fair. Study the original dialogue again before going on.

Vocabulary Exercise 2

Complete each blank space with the appropriate word or words.

It seems that, if you already have money, it's easy to get more. For example, if you've got ——— in ——— and ———, the bank can give you a ——— of, say, 60% of the ——— of your ———.

On the other hand, if you're like the majority of people . . . just managing on your ——— . . . it can be extremely difficult to get even a small ———.

Suppose, for instance, you have to buy a car in a hurry. You need a car for your job, and the one you've got has been written off in an accident. You find one which ——— SFr. 11,500. You can ——— it in ———, but you must make a ——— of SFr. 3,500.

You ——— the ———. You've been a ——— for a very long time, and your ——— for the past eight years has been ——— regularly into a ———. It seems the obvious place to go for a ———. Unfortunately, you find that you have two possibilities: either they can give you a ——— loan – for two to three months, or they can let you have an ——— to the ——— of your ———. You don't earn three and a half thousand a month, and you couldn't possibly ——— such a ——— in three months.

When you've finished, turn over the page and correct what you've done. Then use the following table to interpret your result.

21 or more correct	Excellent
19 or 20 correct	Good
17 or 18 correct	Fair. Study the original dialogue again before going on.

It seems that, if you already have money, it's easy to get more. For example, if you've got investments in bonds and shares, the bank can give you a loan of, say, 60% of the value of your securities.

On the other hand, if you're like the majority of people . . . just managing on your salary . . . it can be extremely difficult to get even a small loan.

Suppose, for instance, you have to buy a car in a hurry. You need a car for your job, and the one you've got has been written off in an accident. You find one which costs SFr. 11,500. You can buy it in instalments, but you must make a down payment of SFr. 3,500.

You approach the bank. You've been a client for a very long time, and your salary for the past eight years has been paid regularly into a deposit account. It seems the obvious place to go for a loan. Unfortunately, you find that you have two possibilities: either they can give you a short-term loan – for two to three months, or they can let you have an overdraft to the value of your salary. You don't earn three and a half thousand a month, and you couldn't possibly pay back such a sum in three months.

Post-test

1 Our affiliated firm can also take out an all-risk ——— for you.

2 Bonds can be sold at any time, and the ——— are fixed daily.

3 Could the bank give me a ——— to cover the down payment?

4 I'll need forty to fifty thousand pounds at ———.

5 Would my wife's power of attorney be ——— on all my accounts?

6 The bank can give you a loan with your life insurance policy as ———.

7 I run a risk if I sell my bonds before they come to ———.

8 I've recently ——— a small amount of capital.

9 Does a deposit account ——— me to a cheque-book?

10 How soon would you like to ——— to your capital once it's been invested?

If you're not sure of any of the answers, look back and check. The fact that you're not sure is as serious as if you were wrong. The answers to this post-test are not given in this book. It's up to you.

5 A mortgage

Objective: To enable you to discuss a mortgage with a client.

Pre-test

Fill in each space with the appropriate word or words.

1 My ———'s in the order of £10,000 a year.

2 The bank's got very good ——— with the organization you work for.

3 The Central Mortgage Agency can lend you the difference between the first mortgage and 80% of the ——— value of the house.

4 To what ——— are you in a position to help me?

5 I think £60,000 is a ——— of the value of the house.

6 My contract will be ——— at least twice.

7 Have you got any other ——— of income besides your salary?

8 I've already had a second ——— concerning the value of the house, and it seems that the price is reasonable.

9 If you'll just fill in this ———, we can send it to the CMA for you.

10 The bank can let you have a first ——— on your house, and the CMA can give you a second.

When you've finished, turn over the page and check your answers. Keep a note of your mark, as you'll need it later to compare it with your result on the post-test.

Answers to Pre-test

1 My income's in the order of £10,000 a year.

2 The bank's got very good relations with the organization you work for.

3 The Central Mortgage Agency can lend you the difference between the first mortgage and 80% of the estimated value of the house.

4 To what extent are you in a position to help me?

5 I think £60,000 is a reasonable estimate of the value of the house.

6 My contract will be renewed at least twice.

7 Have you got any other source of income besides your salary?

8 I've already had a second opinion concerning the value of the house, and it seems that the price is reasonable.

9 If you'll just fill in this form, we can send it to the CMA for you.

10 The bank can let you have a first mortgage on your house, and the CMA can give you a second.

Case 5: A mortgage

Peter MacDonald works with the World Health Organization in Geneva. He started the job two months ago, and is at present looking for a suitable permanent place to live for himself and his family. His wife and children are still in Paris.

His present contract at the WHO is for a minimum of three years, but he has been assured that it will be renewed at least twice.

He has now found a house which seems ideal. It costs £60,000. Peter has about £12,000, and his problem is to find the rest.

He visits George Hudson at the bank to discuss the possibility of getting a mortgage.

Role-playing Exercise

Two people take the roles of MacDonald and Hudson, and act out the case.

Dialogue

Now listen to the tape-recording until you understand it without looking at the text. The terminology on page 49 will help you.

The Form of an Interview

Using the text, divide the interview up into sections as shown on page 16. Then evaluate each part.

Second Role-playing Exercise

Two people take the roles of Hudson and MacDonald, and act out the case without the help of the tape-recording.

Text and Programmed Exercise

Look at the text, and when you're sure you have no problem understanding it, turn to page 50.

MacDonald	Mr Hudson?
Hudson	Yes. Good morning. Come in.
MacDonald	Good morning.
Hudson	Have a seat, please.
MacDonald	Thank you.
Hudson	What can I do for you, Mr MacDonald?
MacDonald	I've been here for two months now. I work with the World Health Organization. Up till now, I've been living in a small apartment that belongs to a friend, and I've been looking round to find somewhere permanent to live. My family's still in Paris, by the way . . . my wife and children. I've recently found a house about twenty minutes from my office, which seems ideal. . . . The price is £60,000. I've got some £12,000, and my problem is to find the rest. The reason I'm here, is to find out to what extent you are in a position to help me.
Hudson	First, I'd like to say that we aren't specialists in mortgages. But as you're a civil servant working for the WHO . . . we can probably help you, in view of our relations with that organization. How long is your contract with the WHO?
MacDonald	Three years minimum, but I've been assured that the contract will be renewed at least twice. Personally, I don't plan to be here all my life, but I think that eight to ten years is a reasonable estimate.
Hudson	What's your position in the organization, Mr MacDonald?
MacDonald	I'm here as a specialist in statistics, and I'm head of a small section. I presume you're interested in my income, however. It's in the order of £10,000 a year, in addition to expenses.
Hudson	Have you got a plan of the house?

MacDonald	A plan . . . no . . . but I can ask the agency to let you have one. It's quite big. . . . It's got five bedrooms, and two living rooms, in addition to the kitchen, laundry, three bathrooms and so on. It's got quite a big garden too . . . oh, and a garage for two cars.
Hudson	What's the total area of the property?
MacDonald	It's about 2,200 square metres.*
Hudson	(writing) About 2,200 square metres. Well, that's quite enough to keep you busy during your free time.
MacDonald	(laughing) Luckily my wife's very energetic, so she'll cut the grass.
Hudson	Good. You have £12,000 at your disposal.
MacDonald	Yes.
Hudson	First of all, we'll have to ask our architect to look at the house, just to see whether the price of £60,000 is reasonable.
MacDonald	Yes, I see. I'm sure your architect will agree with the price. I've already had a second opinion, and I'm told that the price is perfectly reasonable. What I'd like to have is some details on a mortgage. . . .
Hudson	We'll allow you a first mortgage of 50% of the value of the property. In other words, £30,000. Now you say you have £12,000. Have you also got any investments that we could use as collateral?
MacDonald	Yes. I've got some bonds and some shares . . . to a value of some £20,000.
Hudson	We'd be able to lend you 60% of that. That would come to about £12,000. Let's see. £12,000 plus £30,000 plus £12,000 . . . that comes to £54,000. You still need £6,000. There's an organization called the Central Mortgage Agency, which gives second mortgages. They can lend you the difference between the first mortgage and 80% of the estimated value of the house. If we calculate the value of the

house at £50,000 . . . they're always very cautious . . . 80% would be £40,000. If we deduct £30,000 for the first mortgage, that leaves £10,000 . . . just what you need.

MacDonald — Do you do everything necessary to obtain the second mortgage?

Hudson — We'll give you a form to fill in and send it on to the CMA. Shall we just calculate the annual cost such a mortgage would represent?

MacDonald — Certainly.

Hudson — The first mortgage is 7%. That comes to £2,100; the amortization at 2% comes to £600. . . ; the loan against bonds . . . 7% too, that's to say, £840; the 20% lent by the CMA at 7½% comes to £750; the amortization at 6% . . . £600.

Let's just add that up. Nine . . . twenty-eight . . . four. That comes to four thousand eight hundred and ninety pounds a year.

MacDonald — In other words, about £400 a month. . . . That's a lot.

Hudson — Have you got any other source of income?

MacDonald — Yes. My wife has some investments, and I think we'll have to look into that.

I must say, housing is very expensive here.

Hudson — I agree, and the monthly cost of such an operation would be enormous.

MacDonald — Do you think it's *worth* buying a house[1]? Or do I run a risk of a loss when I move on?

Hudson — In general, buying a house insures you against inflation if the price at the start is correct.

MacDonald — Well, thank you for your help. When do you think your surveyor could visit the house?

Hudson — Well, my telephone's 22.84.96. As soon as you have the documents on the house, you can call me, and we can fix an appointment with our architect.

MacDonald — Thank you very much. I'll be calling you in two or three days.

Hudson — Thank *you*.

[1]US: . . . *worth buying a home* is also possible.

Terminology

agency	There's an *agency* which deals with second mortgages.
allow	We'll *allow* you a first mortgage of 50% of the value of the property.
amortization	The *amortization* on the first mortgage comes to £600.
annual cost	The *annual cost* of such an operation is enormous.
area	The total *area* of the property is 2,200 square metres.
assured	I've been *assured* that my contract will be renewed.
cautious	The Central Mortgage Agency are always very *cautious*, so let's say the value of the property is only £50,000.
contract	I've got a three-year *contract* at the NHO.
estimate	I think eight years is a reasonable *estimate* of the length of time I'll be living here.
estimated value	I'm sure your architect will agree with the *estimated value* of the house.
expenses	I earn about £10,000 a year, plus *expenses*.
form	If you fill in this *form*, we can send it to the CMA.
in a position	To what extent are you *in a position* to help me?
inflation	Buying a house insures you against *inflation*.
insures	Buying a house *insures* you against inflation.
mortgage	We can let you have a first *mortgage* of £30,000.
operation	Such an *operation* would mean an enormous annual expense.
outright	I haven't got enough money to buy the house *outright*.
property	What's the value of the *property* you want to buy?
reasonable	Our architect thinks the price you were given for the house is *reasonable*.
relations	The bank's *relations* with the company you work for are good.
renewed	How often do you think your contract will be *renewed*?
represent	What annual cost would such an operation *represent*?
second opinion	Have you had a *second opinion* concerning the value of the property?
source	Have you got any other *source* of income besides your salary?
total	The *total* area of the property I want is 2,200 square metres.
to what extent	I'd like to know *to what extent* you're in a position to help.
value (v)	I've had the property *valued*, and it's worth £66,000.

Programmed Exercise

Hawkins — First of all, we'll have to ask our architect to look at the house, just to see whether the price of £60,000 is reasonable.

MacDonald — Yes, I see.

1 Who will the bank have to ask to look at the house?

. . .

Their architect.

2 Will the bank arrange a mortgage immediately?

. . .

No. First of all, they'l' have to ask their architect to look at the house.

3 Ask Hawkins why their architect will have to look at the house.

. . .

Why will your architect have to look at the house?

4 Why will their architect have to look at the house?

. . .

Just to see whether the price of £60,000 is reasonable.

MacDonald — I'm sure your architect will agree with the price. I've already had a second opinion, and I'm told that the price is perfectly reasonable.

5 What does MacDonald think the architect will do?

. . .

Agree with the price.

6 How can MacDonald be sure the price is reasonable?

. . .

He's already had a second opinion.

7 What has MacDonald been told?

. . .

That the price is perfectly reasonable.

MacDonald	What I'd like to have is some details on a mortgage.
Hawkins	We'll allow you a first mortgage of 50% of the value of the property. In other words, £30,000.

8 What would MacDonald like to have?

. . .

Some details on a mortgage.

9 Why did MacDonald visit the bank?

. . .

Because he'd like to have some details on a mortgage.

10 Ask Hawkins how much the bank can allow for a first mortgage.

. . .

How much can the bank allow for a first mortgage?

11 How much can the bank allow for a first mortgage?

. . .

50% of the value of the property.

Hawkins	You say you have £12,000. Have you also got some investments that we could use as collateral?
MacDonald	Yes. I've got some bonds and some shares . . . to a value of some £20,000.
Hawkins	We'd be able to lend you 60% of that. That would come to £12,000.

12 Ask MacDonald how much he's got.

. . .

How much have you got?

13 What does Hawkins ask MacDonald?

. . .

If he's also got some investments that they could use as collateral.

14 Ask MacDonald what kind of investments he's got.

. . .

What kind of investments have you got?

15 What kind of investments has he got?

. . .

Some bonds and some shares.

You've just answered 15 questions. If you got 2 or more wrong, do them again. If you got 1 or less wrong, go on to the next exercise.

Vocabulary Exercise 1

Fill in each blank space with the word or words that are most appropriate.

Hawkins	There's an ——— called the Central Mortgage Agency, which gives ———. They can ——— you the ——— between the first mortgage and 80% of the ——— of the house. If we ——— the value of the house at £50,000 . . . they're always very ——— . . . 80% would be £40,000. If we ——— £30,000 for the first mortgage, that leave £10,000 . . . just what you need.
MacDonald	Do you do everything necessary to ——— the ———?
Hawkins	We'll give you a ——— to fill in and send it on to the CMA. Shall we just ——— the annual ——— such a ——— would represent?
MacDonald	Certainly.
Hawkins	The first ——— is 7%. That ——— to £2,100; the ——— at 2% comes to £600; the loan ——— bonds . . . 7% too, that's to say, £840; the 20% lent by the CMA at 7½% ——— to £750; the ——— at 6% . . . £600. Let's just ——— that up. Nine . . . twenty-eight . . . four. That ——— to four thousand eight hundred and ninety pounds a year.
MacDonald	In other words, about £400 ———. . . . That's a lot.
Hawkins	Have you got any other ——— of ———?
MacDonald	Yes. My wife has some ———, and I think we'll have to look into that.

When you've finished, turn back to the original text and check your answers. Then use the following table to interpret your result.

25 or more correct	Excellent
Between 22 and 24 correct	Good
Between 19 and 21 correct	Fair. Study the original dialogue again before going on.

Vocabulary Exercise 2

Complete each blank space with the appropriate word or words.

Buying a house is one way of——— against———. Normally, if you find a house that looks suitable, you have it ———. It's a wise idea, particularly if a very large——— is———, to have a second———, just to make sure that the ——— given is———.

Very few people, however, have enough ——— to buy ——— outright. They usually ——— a bank to see about getting a ———. The bank, of course, has to be very careful. They'll need a ——— of the house, and they'll have to ask their own ——— to take a look at it, to ——— the ——— value.

If the bank is ———, they can let you have 50% of the ——— of the ——— as a first———. If this doesn't——— the entire———, they can ——— you 60% of the ——— of any ——— or ——— which you may have. If you still haven't got enough, or if you haven't got any ——— which the bank can use as——— for a second———, then you can go to a specialized organization. They can give you a second———, which will be the ——— between the first one and 80% of the ——— value of the ———.

With the——— and——— on both———, and possibly the——— on a ——— against ———, the annual ——— which such an ——— represents can be very high.

When you've finished, turn over the page and check what you've done. Then use the following table to interpret your result.

35 or more correct	Excellent
Between 31 and 34 correct	Good
Between 28 and 30 correct	Fair. Study the original dialogue again before going on.

Buying a house is one way of insuring against inflation. Normally, if you find a house that looks suitable, you have it valued. It's a wise idea, particularly if a very large sum is involved, to have a second opinion, just to make sure that the price given is reasonable.

Very few people, however, have enough money to buy property outright. They usually approach a bank to see about getting a loan. The bank, of course, has to be very careful. They'll need a plan of the house, and they'll have to ask their own architect to take a look at it, to confirm the estimated value.

If the bank is satisfied, they can let you have 50% of the value of the property as a first mortgage. If this doesn't cover the entire cost, they can lend you 60% of the value of any bonds or shares which you may have. If you still haven't got enough, or if you haven't got any investments which the bank can use as collateral for a second loan, then you can go to a specialized organization. They can give you a second mortgage, which will be the difference between the first one and 80% of the estimated value of the property.

With the interest and amortization on both mortgages, and possibly the interest on a loan against investments, the annual cost which such an operation represents can be very high.

Post-test

Complete each blank space with the appropriate word or words.

1 I haven't got enough in my ——— to cover a down-payment on a car.

2 In general, buying a house ——— you against inflation?

3 What's the total area of the ——— you want to buy?

4 The CMA are always very ———, so we'll estimate the value of the property at £10,000 less than you say.

5 How would you ——— the loan to the bank?

6 We'll have to ask our architect to take a ——— at the house.

7 The monthly cost of such an ——— would be enormous.

8 Is this the department that ——— short-term loans?

9 Have you got any ——— or shares that we could use as collateral?

10 I haven't had the property ——— yet, so I can't even give you estimate of its value.

If you're not sure of any of the answers, look back and check. The fact that you're not sure is as serious as if you were wrong. The answers to this post-test are not given in this book. It's up to you.

6 Refusing a loan

Objective: To enable you to discuss a large loan with a client and to refuse such a loan.

Pre-test

Fill in each space with the appropriate word or words.

1 Your problem may seem simple to you, but in fact it's quite ———.

2 I've been offered ——— in the old part of town, and I'd like to use them to set up an office.

3 I haven't got a ——— residence in this country.

4 You'll need about $50,000 to ——— all initial expenses.

5 I haven't got a cent, so I'll have to ——— the entire amount.

6 Have you got a friend who could put up a ——— for you?

7 The fact that you haven't got a residence permit ——— us from helping you.

8 Under those conditions, we'd have to be entirely ——— before we could help you.

9 I'm afraid the bank couldn't ——— a guarantee of that kind.

10 My ——— tells me that such a project would attract the public.

When you have finished, turn over the page and check your answers. Make a note of your mark, as you'll need to refer to it later.

Answers to Pre-test

1 Your problem may seem simple to you, but in fact it's quite complicated.

2 I've been offered premises in the old part of town, and I'd like to use them to set up an office.

3 I haven't got a permanent residence in this country.

4 You'll need about $50,000 to cover all initial expenses.

5 I haven't got a cent, so I'll have to borrow the entire amount.

6 Have you got a friend who could put up a guarantee for you?

7 The fact that you haven't got a residence permit prevents us from helping you.

8 Under those conditions, we'd have to be entirely covered before we could help you.

9 I'm afraid the bank couldn't accept a guarantee of that kind.

10 My experience tells me that such a project would attract the public.

Case 6: Refusing a loan

Oscar Wills is an American who organizes exhibitions and opens art galleries. He's already organized several exhibitions in Europe, but so far he's never done anything in Switzerland.

Someone has recently offered him premises in the old part of Geneva, and he'd like to set up an art gallery with a permanent exhibition. From experience, he believes that such an operation will attract the public. He and his associates are in contact with a number of galleries, and they sell the works of a dozen or so painters.

He's been in Geneva just one month, at the Intercontinental Hotel, and he intends staying just long enough to set up the gallery. Next week, he has to be in Stockholm, and in eight weeks he's opening another show in Milan.

He needs about $50,000 to cover all the initial expenses. At the moment, he hasn't got a cent, and he visits John Hawkins at the bank to see if he can raise the sum in question. Mr Hawkins has to refuse the loan.

Role-playing Exercise

Two people take the roles of Wills and Hawkins, and act out the case.

Dialogue

Now listen to the tape-recording until you understand it without looking at the text. The terminology on pages 59 and 60 will help you.

The Form of an Interview

Using the text, divide the interview up into sections as shown on page 16. Then evaluate each part.

Second Role-playing Exercise

Two people take the roles of Wills and Hawkins, and act out the case without the help of the tape-recording.

Text and Programmed Exercise

Look at the text, and when you're sure you understand it it, turn to page 61.

Wills	Good morning.
Hawkins	Good morning, sir. Can I take your coat for you?
Wills	Don't worry, I'll put it here. Thank you.
Hawkins	Have a seat.
Wills	Thank you.
Hawkins	What can I do for you?
Wills	Well, it's very simple . . . and complicated. Simple for me, because I know what I want . . . I'm American. I organize exhibitions and open art galleries. I've organized several exhibitions in Europe, but until now, I've never done anything in Switzerland. A short time ago, someone offered me premises – fairly big – in the old part of the town – and I'd like to set up a gallery with a permanent exhibition. . . . And the reason I'm here is I need capital. I'll be quite frank . . . I don't have a cent. My experience tells me that such an operation attracts the public . . . a lot of people are interested in modern painting. . . . We're in contact with a number of galleries, and we sell works of a dozen or so painters. I'd like to know if and how your bank could help me.
Hawkins	First of all, how long have you been living in this country?
Wills	Just one month, but I don't really live here. In fact, next week I have to be in Stockholm for an exhibition, and in eight weeks I'm opening another show in Milan. I travel continually. I'm at the Intercontinental Hotel at the moment. . . . I'm just staying until I set up the gallery.
Hawkins	How much capital do you need at the start?
Wills	I calculate about $50,000 to cover all initial expenses.
Hawkins	And you haven't got anything at all?
Wills	Nothing.

Hawkins	You need to borrow the $50,000.
Wills	Yes.
Hawkins	I'm afraid that, under those conditions, it's difficult for us to help you.
Wills	Oh . . . I see.
Hawkins	. . . if not impossible.
Wills	. . . In that case, I can try another bank. If there is a possibility here, we can study it together.
Hawkins	The only possibility I can see would be to ask a third person to intervene. Have you got any friends who could put up a guarantee?
Wills	I can place about thirty paintings at your disposal as collateral.
Hawkins	I'm afraid we can't accept a guarantee of such a kind. We are not in a position to estimate the value of any painting you place at our disposal.
Wills	So you can't see your way to helping me?
Hawkins	I'm very sorry, but I can't. The simple fact that you have no residence permit prevents us from helping you unless we are entirely covered.
Wills	I understand. Well, thank you for giving me your time.
Hawkins	It's a pleasure. Please come and see me again if ever you need anything . . . and I do wish you the best of luck in your project.
Wills	Thank you.

Terminology

absorb	The discounts he offers *absorb* all his profit.
accept	I'm afraid we can't *accept* paintings as collateral.
back (v)	*Backed* by a commercial guarantee, the bank can let you have a loan.
borrow	I haven't got any money, so I'd like to *borrow* £500.

commercial guarantee	Here's the name of an organization which gives *commercial guarantees* for loans from banks.
entirely covered	As you don't live in this country, we'd have to be *entirely covered* before helping you.
facilities	I'm afraid we'll have to stop your overdraft *facilities*.
guarantee	Have you got a friend who can put up a *guarantee*?
initial expenses	I calculate I'll need £5,000 to cover *initial expenses*.
intervene	The only possibility would be for a third person to *intervene*.
project	I'm sure my *project* will be a big success.
reserve capital	Over the past three years, I've built up a *reserve capital* of about £10,000.
third person	Do you know a *third person* who could give you a guarantee?
tightening up of restrictions	Because of the *tightening up of restrictions* on loans, I'm afraid we'll need a better guarantee than you've got.
turnover	Our *turnover* has increased about 200% in the past year.
under those conditions	I'm afraid, *under those conditions*, we can't help you.

Programmed Exercise

Hawkins	How long have you been living in this country?
Wills	Just one month, but I don't really live here.

1 Ask Wills how long he's been living in this country.

. . .

How long have you been living in this country?

2 How long has he been living here?

. . .

Just one month.

3 Ask Wills if he really lives here, or if he's just passing through.

. . .

Do you really live here, or are you just passing through?

Wills	In fact, next week I have to be in Stockholm for an exhibition, and in eight weeks, I'm opening another show in Milan. I travel continually.

4 Ask Wills if he'll be here next week.

. . .

Will you be here next week?

5 Why won't Wills be here next week?

. . .

Because he has to be in Stockholm for an exhibition.

6 Ask Wills where he'll be in eight weeks' time.

. . .

Where will you be in eight weeks' time?

7 Where will he be in eight weeks' time?

. . .

In Milan.

8 Does Wills travel much?

. . .

Yes. He travels continually.

Wills	I'm at the Intercontinental Hotel at the moment. I'm just staying until I can set up the gallery.

9 How long is Wills going to stay at the Intercontinental Hotel?

. . .

Just until he can set up the gallery.

Hawkins	How much capital do you need at the start?
Wills	I calculate about $50,000 to cover all initial expenses.
Hawkins	And you haven't got anything at all?
Wills	Nothing.
Hawkins	You need to borrow the $50,000.
Wills	Yes.

10 How much capital does Wills need at the start?

. . .

He calculates about $50,000.

11 Why does Wills need $50,000 at the start?

. . .

To cover all initial expenses.

12 Ask Wills if he's got any money at the moment?

. . .

Have you got any money at the moment?

13 How much has Wills got?

. . .

Nothing.
(or)
He hasn't got anything. (US: He doesn't have anything.)

14 Ask Wills how much he'd like to borrow.

. . .

How much would you like to borrow?

15 How much would he like to borrow?

. . .

$50,000.

You've just finished 15 questions. If you got 2 or more wrong, do them again. If you got one or less wrong, go on to the next exercise.

Vocabulary Exercise 1

Fill in each blank space with the appropriate word or words.

Hawkins	The only ——— I can see would be to ask a ——— person to ———. Have you got any friends who could ——— up a ———?
Wills	I can place about thirty paintings at your ——— as ———.
Hawkins	I'm ——— we can't ——— a ——— of such a ———. We are not in a ——— to ——— the ——— of any painting you place at our ———.
Wills	So you can't see your ——— to helping me?
Hawkins	I'm very ———, but I can't. The ——— fact that you have no residence ——— prevents us from ——— you unless we are ——— covered.
Wills	I understand. Well, thank you for giving me your time.
Hawkins	It's a ———. Please come and see me again if ever you ——— anything . . . and I do wish you the ——— of luck in your ———.
Wills	Thank you.

When you have finished, turn back to page 59 and correct what you've done. Then use the following table to interpret your level.

22 or more correct	Excellent
20 or 21 correct	Good
18 or 19 correct	Fair. Study the original dialogue again before going on.

Vocabulary Exercise 2

Complete each blank space with the appropriate word or words.

Henry Watson goes to visit Arthur Peterson at the Overseas Bank. Watson used to know Peterson when he was ——— manager at one of the Bank's offices in the suburbs. At that time, Peterson used to give Watson small ——— facilities. A year ago, however, Peterson moved to the central office, and Watson was not able to ——— the same ——— from Peterson's ———.

Watson imports small office machines. He works with a number of manufacturers in Austria and France. However, with the ——— up of ——— on ———, and difficulties getting people to ——— on time, Watson, who works with a very ——— profit ———, has problems. In addition, in order to get ———, he has recently had to offer ——— that have ——— all his ———.

Peterson looks over Watson's ——— and finds that his ——— has ——— 400% over the last four years. However, he has not built up a reserve ———. Peterson finds it impossible to give Watson the ——— he is asking for, but gives him the name of an organization that gives commercial ——— for ——— from banks. ——— by such an ———, the Overseas Bank could then let Watson have the ——— he needs.

When you've finished, turn over the page and check what you've done. Then use the following table to interpret your result.

21 or more correct	Excellent
19 or 20 correct	Good
17 or 18 correct	Fair. Study the original dialogue again before going on.

Henry Watson goes to visit Arthur Peterson at the Overseas Bank. Watson used to know Peterson when he was branch manager at one of the Bank's offices in the suburbs. At that time, Peterson used to give Watson small overdraft facilities. A year ago, however, Peterson moved to the central office and Watson was not able to obtain the same facilities from Peterson's successor.

Watson imports small office machines. He works with a number of manufacturers in Austria and France. However, with the tightening up of restrictions on loans, and difficulties in getting people to pay on time, Watson, who works with a very narrow profit margin, has problems. In addition, in order to get payments, he has recently had to offer discounts that have absorbed all his profit.

Peterson looks over Watson's accounts and finds that his turnover has increased 400% over the past four years. However, he has not built up a reserve capital. Peterson finds it impossible to give Watson the overdraft he is asking for, but gives him the name of an organization that gives commercial guarantees for loans from banks. Backed by such an organization, the Overseas Bank could then let Watson have the overdraft he needs.

Post-test

1 Under those ———, I'm afraid we can't give you a loan.

2 I need £10,000, but I've only got £2,000 in my account. So I'll have to ——— the rest from the bank.

3 We'd have to be entirely ——— before we could help you.

4 Business is very good. My turnover has ———by 200%.

5 I've built up a reserve ——— of some £7,000.

6 Just to cover the initial ——— of setting up the office, I'll need £3,000.

7 Because of the tightening up of ——— on loans, we'll need a better guarantee than you've got.

8 He doesn't make a lot of money, and he offers such high discounts that they ——— all his profit.

9 I'm afraid we aren't able to ——— the value of your paintings.

10 Have you got a permanent ——— in this country, or are you a visitor?

If you're not sure of any of the answers, look back and check. The fact that you're not sure is as serious as if you were wrong. The answers to this post-test are not given in this book. It's up to you.

7 Complaints

The client's complaint is justified. The bank will do everything it can to put things right.

Objective: To enable you to deal with a complaint when the client is justified.

Pre-test

Complete each blank space with the appropriate word or words.

1 My wife hasn't received the money I asked you to ——— from my account to hers last month.

2 I can't understand the long ——— in sending the money: I've never had any problems before.

3 We've asked our ——— in Torremolinos for an explanation of the delay.

4 I asked for the transfer to be made by ———, so they got it in Spain the same day.

5 Can you please ——— the order in writing.

6 I've often made ——— transfers without any difficulty.

7 We'll do everything we can to see that your wife ——— the transfer as soon as possible.

8 I've looked into the matter, and everything seems to be in ——— this end.

9 Can I have your telephone number so that I can ———?

10 My wife still hasn't received the money I asked you to send her, and I'd like an ———.

When you have finished, turn over the page and check your answers. Keep a note of your mark, so that you can compare it with the post-test later.

Answer to Pre-test

1 My wife hasn't received the money I asked you to transfer from my account to hers last month.

2 I can't understand the long delay in sending the money: I've never had any problems before.

3 We've asked our branch (or: correspondent) in Torremolinos for an explanation of the delay.

4 I asked for the transfer to be made by telex[1], so they got it in Spain the same day.

5 Can you please confirm the order in writing.

6 I've often made similar transfers without any difficulty.

7 We'll do everything we can to see that your wife gets (or: receives) the transfer as soon as possible.

8 I've looked into the matter, and everything seems to be in order this end.[2]

9 Can I have your telephone number so that I can call you back?

10 My wife still hasn't received the money I asked you to send her, and I'd like an explanation.

[1] Also possible: *by wire* (US).
by telegram (UK).
[2] You could also say: *at this end.*

Case 7: Complaints

Six weeks ago, Michael MacDonald asked the Swiss Bank Corporation to transfer Pts. 100,000 to his wife in Torremolinos in Spain. The transfer was dated 30 June. On 28 July, MacDonald rings the bank to ask why the money still hasn't arrived.

Philip Hudson of the Swiss Bank Corporation promises to investigate and to call back with an explanation.

He discovers that everything is in order at the Swiss end. He confirms the order by telex, and asks the bank's correspondent in Torremolinos for an explanation.

He then rings Mr MacDonald to bring him up to date on the situation.

Role-playing Exercise

Two people take the roles of MacDonald and Hudson, and act out the case.

Dialogue

Listen to the recording until you understand it without looking at the text. The terminology on pages 72 and 73 will help you.

The Form of an Interview

Divide the conversation into sections as shown on page 16, using the text. Then evaluate each part.

Second Role-playing Exercise

Two people take the roles of MacDonald and Hudson, and act out the case without the help of the tape-recording.

Text and Programmed Exercise

Look at the text, and when you're sure you have no problem understanding it, turn to page 74.

(Telephone rings.)

Hudson	Swiss Bank Corporation.
MacDonald	Good morning. My name's MacDonald.
Hudson	Good morning, Mr MacDonald.
MacDonald	I asked you to make a transfer six weeks ago to my wife in Torremolinos, and she hasn't received anything yet. The transfer was for Pts. 100,000.
Hudson	What was the date of your transfer?
MacDonald	30 June.
Hudson	30 June.
MacDonald	Today is 28 July. The delay surprises me, as I've often made similar transfers and have never had a problem. The bank I dealt with used to transfer the transfer advice directly to the Banco de España in Torremolinos, and the original to the head office in Madrid. I think if a smaller bank than you can manage, you should be able to.
Hudson	But of course. Did you ask for the transfer to be made by telex?
MacDonald	No, but my bank never used to send a telex.
Hudson	I'll look into the matter straight away. Can I have your telephone number, so I can call you back?
MacDonald	Yes. It's 32.84.96, and please call me back as soon as you can.
Hudson	Certainly.
MacDonald	Goodbye.
Hudson	Goodbye.
MacDonald	Yes.
	. . .
Hudson	Mr MacDonald?
MacDonald	Yes.
Hudson	This is Philip Hudson of the Swiss Bank Corporation.

MacDonald Oh, good.

Hudson I've looked into the matter, and everything seems to be in order this end. I've confirmed the order by telex to our correspondent. You won't have anything to pay, of course.

We've also asked our correspondent in Torremolinos for an explanation. As soon as we have one, I'll call you back to let you know the reasons for the delay.

MacDonald Thank you.

Hudson We'll do everything we can to see that your wife receives the transfer as soon as possible.

MacDonald When do you think you'll know something?

Hudson We should get an answer tomorrow.

Complaints

Answering complaints

Answer promptly, and don't argue or criticize.

If you are in the wrong

1 Admit it.
2 Apologize.
3 Explain the cause.
4 Say what you plan to do.

If you are in the right – but will give way

1 Thank the client for telling you about the problem.
2 Sympathize and avoid criticizing.
3 Tell him what you are going to do.
4 Suggest how to avoid trouble in future.

If you are in the right – and can't give way

1 Thank the client for telling you about the problem.
2 Sympathize and avoid criticizing.
3 State your point of view.
4 Suggest how to avoid trouble in future.

Terminology

answer	We should have an *answer* to our telex tomorrow.
call me back	Can you *call me back* with an explanation?
check up	Can you *check up* and see what the problem is?
correspondent	We've sent a telex to our *correspondent* in Madrid.
delay	My wife hasn't received the money yet, and I can't understand the *delay*.
explanation	I don't know what happened, but I'll call you back as soon as I have an *explanation*.
in order	I've checked, and everything seems to be *in order* at this end.

investigate	I'll *investigate* and ring you back this afternoon.
look into the matter	I'll *look into the matter,* and call you back.
made available	We'll see that the money is *made available* this week.
made out	The transfer order was *made out* correctly.
original	We sent the *original* of the transfer to Madrid.
overseas	As the transfer is to someone *overseas*, it may take us a day or two to find out what the problem is.
reason	Can you find out what the *reason* for the delay is?
receive	We'll do everything possible to make sure your wife *receives* the money this week.
telex	If we send a *telex*, we can have an answer today.
transfer	Six weeks ago, I asked you to *transfer* some money.
transfer advice	My bank always sent the *transfer advice* to Torremolinos.
transfer order	The *transfer order* was made out correctly.

Programmed Exercise

MacDonald	I asked you to make a transfer six weeks ago to my wife in Torremolinos, and she hasn't received anything yet.

1 What did MacDonald do six weeks ago?

. . .

He asked the bank to make a transfer to his wife in Torremolinos.

2 Ask MacDonald how long it is since he asked the bank to make the transfer.

. . .

How long is it since you asked the bank to make the transfer?

3 How long is it since he asked the bank to make the transfer?

. . .

Six weeks.

4 Ask MacDonald who he wanted the transfer made to.

. . .

Who did you want the transfer made to?

5 Ask MacDonald how much money his wife has received.

. . .

How much money has your wife received?

6 How much money has his wife received?

. . .

She hasn't received anything yet.

MacDonald	The transfer was for Pts. 100,000.
Hudson	What was the date of your transfer?
MacDonald	30 June.
Hudson	30 June.
MacDonald	Today is 28 July.

7 Ask MacDonald how much the transfer was for.

. . .

How much was the transfer for?

8 How much was the transfer for?

. . .

Pts. 100,000.

9 Was it a transfer of Swiss francs?

. . .

No. It was a transfer of pesetas. (Or: No, pesetas.)

10 Ask Hudson what date MacDonald made the transfer on.

. . .

What date did MacDonald make the transfer on?

11 What date did MacDonald make the transfer on?

. . .

On 30 June.

MacDonald The delay surprises me, as I've often made similar transfers and have never had a problem.

12 What surprises MacDonald?

. . .

The delay.

13 Ask MacDonald why the delay surprises him.

. . .

Why does the delay surprise you?

14 Why does the delay surprise him?

. . .

He's often made similar transfers and has never had a problem.

15 What has MacDonald often done?

. . .

He's often made similar transfers.

16 Ask MacDonald if he's ever had problems with similar transfers in the past.

. . .

Have you ever had problems with similar transfers in the past?

17 What kind of problems has MacDonald had with similar transfers?

. . .

He's never had a problem with them.

You've just finished 17 questions. If you got 3 or more wrong, do them again. If you got 2 or less wrong, go on to the next exercise.

Vocabulary Exercise 1

Complete each blank space with the appropriate word or words.

Hudson	This is Philip Hudson of the Swiss Bank Corporation.
MacDonald	Oh, good.
Hudson	I've ——— into the ———, and everything seems to be in ——— this end. I've ——— the ——— by ——— to our ———. You won't have anything to ———, of course. We've also asked our ——— in Torremolinos for an ———. As soon as we have one, I'll ——— to let you know the ——— for the ———.
MacDonald	Thank you.
Hudson	We'll do everything we can to see that your wife ——— the ——— as soon as possible.
MacDonald	When do you think you'll know something?
Hudson	We should get an ——— tomorrow.

When you've finished, turn back to page 70 and check what you've done. Then use the following table to interpret your result.

14 or more correct	Excellent
12 or 13 correct	Good
10 or 11 correct	Fair. Study the original dialogue again before going on.

Writing Exercise

Write a confirmation of Philip Hudson's telephone call.

Vocabulary Exercise 2

Complete each blank space with the appropriate word or words.

It's often very difficult to remain calm and polite when a client ———. However, it's extremely ——— not to get annoyed. You should try to ——— what the problem is. After all, it may be the bank's ———. If it is, the client has a ——— to be angry. If it isn't, it ——— the bank's ——— if an employee is impatient with a client.

Suppose the trouble is that the ——— asked for a ——— to be made to his wife. He did this more than a month ago, but his wife still hasn't ——— the ———. Naturally, he'd like to know the reason for the ———.

You ———, and you find that the ——— order was made out correctly. Therefore, the ——— is not the client's ———. As the ——— is being made to a person overseas, it will probably take you some time to ——— out where the problem lies. In this case, you can immediately ——— to the ——— for the ———. You can then promise to investigate , and to let him know as soon as you have an ———. You must also do everything possible to make sure that the ——— is ——— without any further ———.

When you've finished, turn to the next page and correct what you've done. Then use the following table to interpret your result.

21 or more correct	Excellent
19 or 20 correct	Good
17 or 18 correct	Fair. Study the original dialogue again before going on.

It's often very difficult to remain calm and polite when a client complains. However, it's extremely important not to get annoyed. You should try to find out what the problem is. After all, it may be the bank's fault. If it is, the client has a right to be angry. If it isn't, it damages the bank's image if an employee is impatient with a client.

Suppose the trouble is that the client asked for a transfer to be made to his wife. He did this more than a month ago, but his wife still hasn't received the money. Naturally, he'd like to know the reason for the delay.

You check up, and you find that the transfer order was made out correctly. Therefore, the delay is not the client's fault. As the transfer is being made to a person overseas, it will probably take you some time to find out where the problem lies. In this case, you can immediately apologise to the client for the delay. You can then promise to investigate, and to let him know as soon as you have an explanation. You must also do everything possible to make sure that the money is made available without any further delay.

Post-test

Complete each blank space with the appropriate word or words.

1 My wife still hasn't ——— the money I asked you to send her.

2 What's the ——— for the long delay?

3 Can you look into the ——— and let me know what the problem is?

4 My last bank never made a transfer by———.

5 We sent the ——— of the transfer advice to our head office.

6 I've checked, and everything seems to be in ——— this end.

7 Can you ——— with an explanation? My number is 345550.

8 I sent a telex to our correspondent this morning, so we should get an ——— this afternoon.

9 On 30 June, I asked you to ——— a transfer to my wife in Torremolinos.

10 I can't give you an ——— at the moment, I'm afraid. But I'll look into the matter and call you back with one.

If you're not sure of any of the answers, look back and check. The fact that you're not sure is as serious as if you were wrong. The answers to this post-test are not given in this book. It's up to you.

8 Complaints

The client has made a mistake. However, the bank will put things right.

Objective: To enable you to deal with a complaint where the client has made a mistake, but where the bank is prepared to help.

Pre-test

Complete each blank space with the appropriate word or words.

1 173.227/1. That's an ——— with our main office.

2 We could never get round to ——— every number each client gave us.

3 I'm afraid I inverted the last two ——— of the account.

4 You made a ——— in the number, sir. It should be 272, not 227.

5 Could you ——— the matter and call me back?

6 I want to make a transfer, but I don't know the ——— account number.

7 As our ——— are dealt with electronically, we only take the number into consideration.

8 I've just received the ——— for the transfer I asked you to make last week.

9 We make every effort to ——— a client to let him know when we can't make a payment.

10 I'll send you a letter ——— this conversation.

When you have finished, turn over the page and check your answers. Keep a note of your result, as you'll need to refer to it later.

Answers to Pre-test

1 173.227/1. That's an account with our main office.

2 We could never get round to checking every number each client gave us.

3 I'm afraid I inverted the last two numbers of the account.

4 You made a mistake in the number, sir. It should be 272, not 227.

5 Could you look into the matter and call me back?

6 I want to make a transfer, but I don't know the beneficiary's account number.

7 As our payment orders are dealt with electronically, we only take the number into consideration.

8 I've just received the debit advice for the transfer I asked you to make last week.

9 We make every effort to contact (or call) a client to let him know when we can't make a payment.

10 I'll send you a letter confirming this conversation.

Case 8: Complaints

Henry Williamson is a client of the bank. He asked them to transfer $3,500 to Prosello Incorporated. Prosello has just telephoned him.[1] They are furious because they haven't received the money. However, Williamson has received a debit advice for $3,500 dated 15 July. He rings the bank for an explanation.

Philip Hudson takes all the necessary details, and promises to ring Williamson back as soon as he has an explanation. When he investigates, he finds that Williamson inverted two numbers in Prosello's account number when he filled out the transfer order. When he explains this, Williamson asks him to put things right at the bank, and says that he'll telephone Prosello.

Role-playing Exercises

Two people take the roles of Williamson and Hudson, and act out the two conversations.

Dialogue

Now listen to the tape-recording until you understand it without looking at the text. The terminology on page 84 will help you.

The Form of an Interview

Using the text, divide the interview up into sections as shown on page 16. Then evaluate each part.

Second Role-playing Exercise

Two people take the roles of Williamson and Hudson, and act out the case without the help of the tape-recording.

Text and Programmed Exercise

Look at the text, and when you're sure you have no problem understanding it, turn to page 85.

[1] UK: *Prosello have just telephoned him.*

(Telephone call from a client, Williamson, to Hudson in Transfers. Time: 9.25 a.m.)

Hudson	Transfers.
Williamson	Good morning. This is Henry Williamson.
Hudson	Good morning, Mr Williamson.
Williamson	I'm a client of the bank. My account number is 151.223.
Hudson	Yes, sir.
Williamson	I've just received a debit advice[1] of 15 July.
Hudson	Yes. For what amount?
Williamson	\$3,500.
Hudson	\$3,500.
Williamson	I asked you to transfer this sum to Prosello Incorporated. Prosello has just telephoned me.[2] They're furious. Apparently, they haven't received the transfer. This puts me in a very nasty situation.
Hudson	Could you give me Prosello's address?
Williamson	Yes. 32 East 42nd Street. I've got your debit advice, but they haven't received anything.
Hudson	Have you got the debit advice in front of you, sir?
Williamson	Yes.
Hudson	What's the beneficiary's bank, sir?
Williamson	Yourselves, too.
Hudson	Ourselves.

[1] Also possible: *debit notice*.
[2] UK: *Prosello have just telephoned me.*

Williamson	Their account number's 173.227.
Hudson	173.227.
Williamson	Stroke one.
Hudson	Stroke one. It's an account with our main office. The situation is surprising. I'm going to look into the matter, and I'll call you back. Could I have your number, please?
Williamson	425-9036.
Hudson	425-9036.
Williamson	Can you call me back this morning, please?
Hudson	I'll do what I can, sir.
Williamson	Can I have your name, please?
Hudson	Hudson.
Williamson	Hudson . . . ah.
Hudson	I'll call you back, sir.
Williamson	Thank you. Goodbye.
Hudson	Goodbye, sir.

(Telephone call from Hudson in Transfers to a client, Williamson. Time: 2.42 p.m.)

Williamson	Williamson.
Hudson	This is the Swiss Bank Corporation. Philip Hudson.
Williamson	Oh, good afternoon, Mr Hudson. Have you managed to clear up my case?
Hudson	Yes. It's really quite simple. On your order, you made a mistake in the account number of Prosello. Their account number is 173.272, and you put 173.227, with the last two numbers inverted.

Williamson	Oh, damn.
Hudson	As our payment orders are dealt with electronically, it's the number that is taken. Of course, the person who received the transfer should have noticed. In this case, the beneficiary is a large industry which receives dozens of transfers a day, and they are probably checking up on this one.
Williamson	Oh, fine.
Hudson	In that case, I'll leave it to you to . . .
Williamson	Yes, yes.
Hudson	. . . to telephone Prosello.
Williamson	Yes, but the name was correct.
Hudson	I'm afraid we could simply never get round to checking every number each client gave us.
Williamson	Yes, you're right. Look, please put things right as soon as you can, and I'll call Prosello.
Hudson	Thank you, Mr Williamson.
Williamson	Goodbye.
Hudson	Good afternoon.

Terminology

account number	What's the beneficiary's *account number*, please?
beneficiary	I want to make a transfer, but I don't know the *beneficiary's* address.
checking	We could never get round to *checking* the numbers.
debit advice	I've got the *debit advice* for the transfer I asked you to make.
electronically	We deal with our payment orders *electronically*.
inconvenience	I'm sorry you've been caused this *inconvenience*.
invert	I'm afraid I *inverted* the last two numbers of the account.
mistake	You made a *mistake* on the order.
payment order	We deal with our *payment orders* electronically.
put things right	Can you *put things right* as soon as possible, please.
trace (n)	We can find no *trace* of your order.

Programmed Exercise

Williamson	I'm a client of the bank. My account number is 151.223.
Hudson	Yes.

1 What contact has Williamson got with the bank?

. . .

He's a client.

2 Ask Williamson if he's a client at this branch of the bank.

. . .

Are you a client of this branch of the bank?

Williamson	I've just received a debit advice of 15 July.
Hudson	Yes. For what amount?
Williamson	$3,500.

3 What's Williamson just received?

. . .

A debit advice.

4 Ask Williamson how much the debit advice is for.

. . .

How much is the debit advice for?

5 How much is the debit advice for?

. . .

$3,500.

6 Ask Williamson what the date of the debit advice is.

. . .

What's the date of the debit advice?

Williamson	I asked you to transfer this sum to Prosello Incorporated. Prosello has just telephoned me. They're furious.

7 What did Williamson ask the bank to do with $3,500?

. . .

To transfer it to Prosello Incorporated.

8 Ask Williamson who he's just had a telephone call from.

. . .

Who have you just had a telephone call from?

9 What has Prosello Incorporated just done?

. . .

They've just telephoned Williamson.

Williamson	Apparently, they haven't received the transfer. This puts me in a very nasty situation.

10 What's Williamson's problem?

. . .

Apparently Prosello Incorporated hasn't received the transfer.

11 Why is Williamson in a nasty situation?

. . .

Because Prosello Incorporated hasn't received the transfer.

12 Prosello hasn't received the transfer. What's the result of this?

. . .

Williamson's in a very nasty situation.

Hudson	Could you give me Prosello's address?
Williamson	Yes, 32 East 42nd Street. I've got your debit advice, but they haven't received anything.
Hudson	Have you got the debit advice in front of you, sir?
Williamson	Yes.
Hudson	What's the beneficiary's bank?
Williamson	Yourselves.

13 Ask Williamson for Prosello's address.

. . .

Could you give me Prosello's address?

14 Ask Williamson if he's got the debit advice in front of him.

. . .

Have you got the debit advice in front of you?

15 Ask Williamson who the beneficiary is.

. . .

Who's the beneficiary?

16 Who's the beneficiary?

. . .

Prosello Incorporated.

17 Ask Williamson for the beneficiary's bank.

. . .

What's the beneficiary's bank?

You've just finished 17 questions. If you got 3 or more wrong, do them again. If you got 2 or less wrong, go on to the next exercise.

Vocabulary Exercise 1

Complete each blank space with the appropriate word or words.

Williamson	Have you ——— to clear up my case?
Hudson	Yes. It's really quite simple. On your ———, you made a ——— in the ——— of Prosello. Their ——— is 173.272, and you put 173.227, with the last two numbers ———.
Wiiliamson	Oh, damn.
Hudson	As our ——— are dealt with ———, it's the ——— that is taken. Of course, the person who ——— the ——— should have noticed. In this case, the ——— is a large industry which ——— dozens of ——— a day, and they are probably ——— on this one.
Williamson	Oh, fine.
Hudson	In that case, I'll leave it to you to . . .
Williamson	Yes, yes.
Hudson	. . . to telephone Prosello.
Williamson	Yes, but the name was correct.
Hudson	I'm afraid we could simply never get round to ——— every ——— each ——— gave us.
Williamson	Yes, you're right. Look, please ——— as soon as you can, and I'll call Prosello.
Hudson	Thank you, Mr Williamson.

When you've finished, turn back to pages 83 and 84 and correct what you've done. Then use the following table to interpret your result.

18 or more correct	Excellent
16 or 17 correct	Good
14 or 15 correct	Fair. Study the original dialogue again before going on.

Writing Exercise

Write a letter for Hudson confirming his call.

Vocabulary Exercise 2

Complete each blank space with the appropriate word or words.

On 10 January, John Conway telephones Martin Webster at the bank. His accountant sent an ——— to pay £9,300 to Binglesey Ltd. on 5 December. The Manager of Binglesey has just telephoned him to ——— that this ——— has not yet been made. Conway would like to know why the ——— didn't ——— him to let him know of the ———.

Webster explains that, under normal circumstances, the bank would immediately ——— a ——— if they couldn't make a ———. He promises to ——— and to telephone Conway with an ——— the next morning.

The following morning, Webster telephones Conway to say that the bank can find no ——— of his ———. As it was sent shortly before Christmas, it may have got lost in the post. Mr Conway continues to ———, and Mr Webster says that it's a pity his accountant didn't ——— the bank as soon as he noticed the ——— hadn't been made. This ——— of problem is very quickly put right, and they might have spared Mr Conway any ———. He asks Conway to give him the ———, and promises to make the ——— immediately. Conway agrees to send another ——— this.

When you've finished, turn over the page and check what you've done. Then use the following table to interpret your result.

19 or more correct	Excellent
17 or 18 correct	Good
15 or 16 correct	Fair. Study the original dialogue again before going on.

On 10 January, John Conway telephones Martin Webster at the bank. His accountant sent an order to pay £9,300 to Binglesey Ltd. on 5 December. The Manager of Binglesey has just telephoned him to complain that this payment has not yet been made. Conway would like to know why the bank didn't contact him to let him know of the delay.

Webster explains that, under normal circumstances, the bank would immediately contact a client if they couldn't make a payment. He promises to investigate and to telephone Conway with an explanation the next morning.

The following morning, Webster telephones Conway to say that the bank can find no trace of his order. As it was sent shortly before Christmas, it may have got lost in the post. Mr Conway continues to complain, and Mr Webster says that it's a pity his accountant didn't contact the bank as soon as he noticed the payment hadn't been made. This type of problem is very quickly put right, and they might have spared Mr Conway any inconvenience. He asks Conway to give him the details, and promises to make the payment immediately. Conway agrees to send another order confirming this.

Post-test

Complete each blank space with the appropriate word or words.

1 I want to make a transfer, but I don't know the ——— bank.

2 We deal with our ——— orders electronically.

3 I've checked, but I can find no ——— of this transfer.

4 This delay is ——— us a lot of inconvenience.

5 What's your telephone number, sir? I'll ——— with an explanation.

6 I'll leave it to the bank to ——— things right, then.

7 I think I made a ——— on an order this afternoon. I may have inverted the first two numbers of the account.

8 Mr Waters has only ——— £1,000, but the order was for £3,000.

9 I'm afraid I can't find the debit ——— for our last transfer.

10 I couldn't get ——— to checking all the accounts today.

If you're not sure of any of the answers, look back and check. The fact that you're not sure is as serious as if you were wrong. The answers to this post-test are not given in this book. It's up to you.

9 Complaints

The cause of the complaint is out of both the client's and the bank's control.

Objective: To enable you to deal with a complaint where the bank is not in a position to help the client.

Pre-test

Complete each blank space with the appropriate word or words.

1 While there is a general ——— affecting all investments, I believe that the situation is getting better.

2 He wants to ——— about the drop in the value of his investments.

3 I've just received my ——— of account for the last six months, and I'm very disappointed.

4 You still have gilt-edged ———.

5 Do you think the situation is going to ——— in the near future?

6 I've seen my capital depreciate, while I had hoped at least to keep it ———.

7 If you ——— this statement with your last one, you'll see that all rates have risen considerably.

8 I depend on you to ——— the value of my capital. I don't want to lose money.

9 ——— is possible now, which wasn't the case last year.

10 I hope the next time I come here my investments will have ——— their original value.

When you have finished, turn over the page and correct what you've done. Keep a note of your result, as you'll need to refer to it later.

Answers to Pre-test

1 While there is a general recession affecting all investments, I believe that the situation is getting better.

2 He wants to complain about the drop in the value of his investments.

3 I've just received my statement of account for the last six months, and I'm very disappointed.

4 You still have gilt-edged securities.

5 Do you think the situation is going to improve in the near future?

6 I've seen my capital depreciate, while I had hoped at least to keep it stable.

7 If you compare this statement with your last one, you'll see that all rates have risen considerably.

8 I depend on you to maintain (or: preserve) the value of my capital. I don't want to lose money.

9 Speculation is possible now, which wasn't the case last year.

10 I hope the next time I come here my investments will have regained their original value.

Case 9: Complaints

Alan Connolly has just received his bank statement, and is extremely upset to discover that his capital has depreciated over the past year. He visits the bank and discusses the problem with Charles Finch. He explains that, when he invested his money with the bank, it was because he realized that his French securities were a risk. He had hoped to keep his capital stable. He feels that, although the bank gave him advice about what to buy, he wasn't kept sufficiently informed and wasn't offered the possibility of coping with devalution.

Finch points out that the general recession has affected the whole world, and that the bank's choice of investments in Swiss francs and marks was the best at the time. Connolly still has gilt-edged securities, and compared with the position at the end of the previous year, all rates have risen considerably. Finch says he believes the situation is improving, and that it's merely a question of being patient.

Connolly is pleased to hear that speculation is possible again. He asks Finch to keep him fully informed of events, and then invites him to lunch.

Role-playing Exercise

Two people take the roles of Finch and Connolly, and act out the case.

Dialogue

Now listen to the tape-recording until you understand it without looking at the text. The terminology on pages 95 and 96 will help you.

The Form of an Interview

Using the text, divide the interview up into sections as shown on page 16. Then evaluate each part.

Second Role-playing Exercise

Two people take the roles of Finch and Connolly and act out the case without the help of the tape-recording.

Text and Programmed Exercise

Look at the text, and when you're sure you have no problem understanding it, turn to page 97.

Finch — How are you, Mr Connolly? I'm very pleased to see you.

Connolly — I'm fine, but I must say I'm not too pleased with how things are going.

Finch — Oh? I'm very sorry to hear that. Why?

Connolly — Well, I've just received my statement, and I must say I'm very disappointed. I invested my capital in your bank some time ago, and now I see that rather than having made a profit, I've lost a considerable amount. What's happened over the last year?

Finch — I'm sure you fully understand the general recession that's affecting the whole world. This has necessarily had a negative effect on the stock exchange. I'm sure you can't reproach the bank with having failed you. Our choice was the best at the time. You still have gilt-edged securities, but even our own shares have been affected by the general depression. On the other hand, I'm sure you must be pleased that we bought securities for you in Swiss francs and in marks, while you brought us French francs. If you calculate what you have today – despite the drop in value of the shares and bonds that we bought for you – I'm sure you can't help being pleased. If you had kept your capital in French money, your loss would have been much greater.

Connolly — Yes. I agree. But if I came here, it was because I realized that, by keeping French securites, I ran a risk. Nevertheless, I've seen my capital depreciate, whereas at least I hoped to keep it stable. You gave me advice concerning what to buy. However, I feel you haven't kept me sufficiently informed, and haven't offered me the possibility of coping with devaluation. I understand that there is a general crisis at the moment – that things are different now – but it's no good just sitting back and watching things happen. We have to do something. Do you think the situation is going to improve in the near future?

Finch — I have here an up-to-date statement concerning your securities. If you compare it with the one you received giving you the position at the end of last year, you will see that all rates have risen considerably. I believe we are moving up again, and it's merely a question of being patient. We can't expect miracles, but I'd advise you not to change your present investments. You mentioned a few minutes ago that you thought I should have done something about your investments. This was practically impossible, as all securities, without exception, dropped in value. There was nothing we could do about it. We do everything we can in our clients' interest, but we can't perform miracles.

Connolly So, according to you, I should wait and see.

Finch I think so. The proof is in the present situation of your portfolio.

Connolly Yes. Certainly there's an improvement when you compare with the end of last year. Nevertheless, its very annoying to be a year behindhand, and I'm certain I'm not the only person to point this out to you.

Connolly I have to admit you're quite correct. However, I think you can be confident that we will obtain the best value for your money, as now speculation is possible, which wasn't the case last year.

Connolly That's interesting. Then I depend on you to maintain the value of my capital. I hope that next time I come here I'll see my investment has regained its original value. I'd also be grateful if you could keep me informed of events.

Finch Certainly. We'll take particular care of your portfolio. I'll have it looked into, and according to the proposals that our specialists make, we'll do everything we can.

Connolly Thank you. As my next appointment is this afternoon, can I invite you to have lunch with me?

Finch That's very kind of you. It'd be a pleasure.

Terminology

crisis	There's a general *crisis* at the moment.
depreciate	I've seen my capital *depreciate* in value.
devaluation	I couldn't cope with *devaluation*.
exception	All securities, without *exception*, dropped in value.
gilt-edged	You still have *gilt-edged* securities.
maintain	Can you *maintain* the value of my capital?

meeting commitments	We're having difficulties *meeting* our *commitments*.
original value	How soon will my investments regain their *original value*?
profit	Instead of making a *profit,* I've lost my money.
recession	The general *recession* is affecting the whole world.
reduced staff	During the holidays, we operate with a *reduced staff*.
regain	Your securities have *regained* their original value.
reproach	I'm sure you can't *reproach* the bank.
RTB system	Our new *RTB system* will improve efficiency.
securities	I've got some gilt-edged *securities*.
speculation	*Speculation* is possible now.
stable	I had hoped at least to keep my capital *stable.*
statement	I've just received my *statement*.
up-to-date	Can I have an *up-to-date* statement of account?
work load	We always have a heavy *work load* at the end of the year.

Programmed Exercise

Connolly — If I came here, it was because I realized that, by keeping French securities, I ran a risk.

1 Why did Connolly come to this bank in the first place?

. . .

Because he realized that, by keeping French securities, he ran a risk.

2 In keeping French securities, what did Connolly do?

. . .

He ran a risk.

3 Ask Connolly what kind of investments he had when he came to the bank.

. . .

What kind of investments did you have when you come to the bank?

4 What kind of investments did he have?

. . .

French securities.

Connolly — Nevertheless, I've seen my capital depreciate, whereas at least I hoped to keep it stable.

5 What did Connolly hope to do when he came to this bank?

. . .

To keep his capital stable.

6 And what's happened?

. . .

He's seen his capital depreciate.

Connolly — You gave me advice concerning what to buy. However, I feel that you haven't kept me sufficiently informed, and haven't offered me the possibility of coping with devaluation.

7 What did the bank do?

. . .

Gave Connolly advice concerning what to buy.

8 Is Connolly satisfied with the information the bank has given him?

. . .

No. He feels they haven't kept him sufficiently informed.

9 Does he just feel that they haven't kept him sufficiently informed?

. . .

No. He also feels that they haven't given him the possibility of coping with devaluation.

Connolly I understand that there is a general crisis at the moment – that things are different now – but it's no good just sitting back and watching things happen. We have to do something.

10 What's the problem at the moment?

. . .

There's a general crisis.

11 What does Connolly seem to feel the bank has been doing?

. . .

Just sitting back and watching things happen.

Connolly Do you think the situation is going to improve in the near future?

Finch I have here an up-to-date statement concerning your securities. If you compare it with the one you received giving you the position at the end of last year, you will see that all rates have risen considerably.

12 Ask Finch if the situation will improve soon.

. . .

Will the situation improve soon?

13 What has Finch got?

. . .

An up-to-date statement concerning Connolly's securities.

14 Ask Finch what the position's like compared with that of last year.

. . .

What's the position like compared with that of last year?

15 Ask Connolly if the position now is the same as it was last year.

. . .

Is the position now the same as it was last year?

16 Is the position the same as it was last year?

. . .

No. All rates have risen considerably.

You're just finished 16 questions. If you got 3 or more wrong, do them again. If you got 2 or less wrong, go on to the next exercise.

Vocabulary Exercise 1

Complete each blank space with the appropriate word or words.

Finch I'm sure you fully ——— the general ——— that is ——— the whole world. This has necessarily had a ——— effect on the ———. I'm sure you can't ——— the bank with having failed you. Our ——— was the best at the time. You still have ——— securities, but even our own ——— have been ——— by the general depression.

On the other hand, I'm sure you must be pleased that we bought ——— for you in Swiss francs and in marks, while you ——— us French francs. If you ——— what you have today – ——— the drop in ——— of the ——— and ——— that we bought for you – I'm sure you can't help being pleased. If you had ——— your ——— in French money, your ——— would have been much ———.

Connolly Yes, I agree. But if I came here, it was because I ——— that by ——— French ———, I ran a ———. Nevertheless, I've seen my capital ———, whereas at least I hoped to keep it ———.

When you've finished, turn back to page 94 and correct what you've done. Then use the following table to interpret your level.

24 or more correct	Excellent
22 or 23 correct	Good
20 or 21 correct	Fair. Study the original dialogue again before going on.

Vocabulary Exercise 2

Complete each blank space with the appropriate word or words.

Francis Reynolds telephones the bank to ——— about a delay in ——— a payment. The ——— put him through to Christopher Jones, and Reynolds ——— that he ——— the transfer order personally on 16 December. This was a ——— for goods which were needed urgently. However, as the ——— was not ——— until 28 December, the goods were not shipped, and now his company is having serious ——— meeting commitments.

Jones ——— the problem and calls Reynolds back later that day. The ——— was ——— the bank's ——— due to the very heavy work ——— at the end of the year. Also, because of Christmas ———, they were ——— with a ——— staff. The bank is, in addition, ——— a new RTB ———. This will, in the long run, improve ———, but for the first couple of months ——— can cause ———.

When you've finished, turn over the page and correct what you've done. Then use the following table to interpret your result.

19 or more correct	Excellent
17 or 18 correct	Good
15 or 16 correct	Fair. Study the original dialogue again before going on.

Francis Reynolds telephones the bank to complain about a delay in making a payment. The operator puts him through to Christopher Jones, and Reynolds explains that he made out the transfer order personally on 16 December. This was a payment for goods which were needed urgently. However, as the money was not received until 28 December, the goods were not shipped, and now his company is having serious difficulties meeting commitments.

Jones investigates the problem and calls Reynolds back later that day. The delay was entirely the bank's fault, due to the very heavy work load at the end of the year. Also, because of Christmas holidays, they were operating with a reduced staff. The bank is, in addition, introducing a new RTB system[1]. This will, in the long run, improve efficiency, but for the first couple of months this can cause delays.

[1] Real Time Banking.

Post-test

Complete each blank space with the appropriate word or words.

1 You still have gilt-edged ———.

2 Despite the ——— in the value of what we bought for you, I'm sure you can't help being pleased.

3 All securities dropped in value because of the ———.

4 I consolidated all my ——— in your bank some time ago.

5 I don't think you can ——— the bank with having failed you.

6 The delay was ——— to the very heavy work load.

7 Far from making a ———, I've actually lost money.

8 In the long run, the new RTB system will improve ———.

9 We haven't received the money yet, and we're having serious difficulties ——— our commitments.

10 In keeping French securities, you run a very serious ———.

If you're not sure of any of the answers, look back and check. The fact that you're not sure is as serious as if you were wrong. The answers to this post-test are not given in this book. It's up to you.

Terminology

A

absorb (6)
accept (6)
access (have access to) (1)
account (1)
account number (8)
acquired (1)
affiliated (4)
agency (5)
allow (5)
all-risk (4)
amount (1)
amortization (5)
annual cost (5)
answer (7)
area (5)
assets(3)
assured (5)
at your disposal (1)
available (1)

B

back (v) (6)
balance (4)
beneficiary (8)
block (1)
bond (3)
borrow (6)

C

call me back (7)
capital (1)
cautious (5)
certificate of deposit (1)
checkbook (US) (1)
cheque-book (UK) (1)
checking (8)
checking account (US) (1)
check-up (7)
collateral (3)
commercial guarantee (6)
consolidate (3)
contract (5)
correspondent (7)
counter (UK) (1)
cover (4)
crisis (9)
current account (UK) (1)

D

deal with (4)
debit advice (8)
deduction (4)
delay (7)
deposit (1)
deposit account (UK) (1)
depreciate (9)
devaluation (9)
disposal (1)
diversify (3)
dividend (3)
down payment (4)

E

electronically (8)
entirely covered (6)
entitle (1)
estimate (5)
estimated value (5)
exception (9)
expenses (5)
explanation (7)
extent, to what (5)

F

facilities (6)
finance firm (4)
fixed period (3)
fixed rate (3)
fluctuation (3)
form (5)
funds (3)

G

gilt-edged (9)
guarantee (6)

H

have access to (1)

I

in a position (5)
inconvenience (8)
inflation (5)
inheritance (3)
initial expenses (6)
in order (7)
instalments (4)
insurance (4)
insures (5)
interest (1)
intervene (6)
invert (8)
invest (1)
investigate (7)
investment (1)
investment department (1)
investment fund (3)
issue (3)

L

limit (1)
loan (3)
long-term (1)
look into the matter (7)
loss (3)

M

made available (7)
made out (7)
maintain (9)
market (3)